JAPANESE AIRCRAFT
OF WORLD WAR II
1937–1945

JAPANESE AIRCRAFT
OF WORLD WAR II
1937–1945

THOMAS NEWDICK

Reprinted in 2018, 2020, 2021 and 2023

Published by Amber Books Ltd
United House
London N7 9DP
United Kingdom
www.amberbooks.co.uk
Instagram: amberbooksltd
Facebook: amberbooks
Twitter: @amberbooks
Pinterest: amberbooksltd

ISBN: 978-1-78274-474-0

Editor: Michael Spilling
Designer: Andrew Easton
Picture research: Terry Forshaw

Printed in China

Picture Credits:
Alamy: 88/89 (Aviation History Collection)
Art-Tech/Aerospace: 7, 26, 30/31, 54/55, 95, 100, 114, 115, 119, 121, 123
Cody Images: 6, 8/9, 16, 21, 39, 64, 69, 71, 74, 80, 84, 91
U S Department of Defense: 76/77

All artworks © Art-Tech/Aerospace except 18, 19, 43, 86, 92 all © Vincent Bourguignon

Contents

Introduction

From modest origins, the air power of the Imperial Japanese Army and Navy rapidly developed during the interwar period, but after a string of successes in battle against China and then in the Pacific War, the tide turned decisively against it from mid-1942.

The Imperial Japanese Army first employed balloons in the 1870s, and these saw action against Russian forces during the Russo-Japanese War. In 1910 the Japanese Army sent its first pilots to Europe for training in heavier-than-air flight. This initial cadre returned to Japan the same year, bringing the first aircraft for the Army. In 1919 an Army Air Division was formally established and was provided with initial equipment of French origin. In 1925 this formation was succeeded by the Army Air Corps, which soon began

to receive the first military aircraft of Japanese design and manufacture.

The Army Air Division/Corps saw early combat against Russia in 1920 and then against China in the Tsinan Incident of 1928. From then on, the aircraft of the Imperial Japanese Army (IJA) would see intensive combat use, beginning with the Manchurian Incident in 1931 and the Shanghai Incident a year later. Now employing primarily Japanese equipment, the Air Division/Corps quickly achieved supremacy over the Chinese. These successes

prompted a wholesale programme of re-equipment and strengthening of forces, coinciding with the next major conflict, the Second Sino-Japanese War that began in 1937. It was during this conflict, in which the aircraft of the IJA were primarily employed for ground support of troops, that the structure and tactics were established for the

The mainstay of the Imperial Japanese Navy bomber arm for most of the Pacific War, the Mitsubishi G4M offered excellent range but was vulnerable when confronted by opposition fighters.

forthcoming Pacific War. Aircraft of the IJA were also blooded in action against Russia during the border incidents at Changkufeng and Nomonhan. These battles led to an increasing emphasis on short-range operations over land, which would have an impact on the coming war against the Allies.

At the outbreak of the Pacific War in December 1941 it was the aircraft of the Imperial Japanese Navy that led the line, beginning with the devastating attack against the US Navy anchorage at Pearl Harbor.

Aviation pioneers
The origins of the IJN had been laid down in 1912 and the air arm saw some action in the course of World War I before launching its first ship-borne operations in the early 1920s. As a pioneer of carrier aviation, the IJN was well placed to do battle with Chinese forces during incidents in the 1920s and 1930s, culminating in the Second Sino-Japanese War. As well as the carriers, the IJN scored successes in long-range attacks by land-based bombers. Drawing upon lessons learned in battle against China, both these elements would again be at

Nakajima Ki-43-Ic fighters of the 50th Sentai, based at Tokorozawa in June 1942. Typical of early-war Japanese fighters, the 'Oscar' starred in initial successes before its lack of firepower and limited protection began to be found wanting against better equipped opposition.

the forefront of first Japanese military operations against the Allies, during which the IJN bore the brunt of the initial fighting in the air.

In the opening nine months of the war in the Pacific, the Japanese emerged victorious in a succession of campaigns, with IJA and IJN air power proving generally superior to anything the Allies had in theatre. However, by July 1942 Japanese expansion had reached its limits, and what followed would be a war of attrition, seeing mounting Japanese losses between autumn 1942 and October 1944.

Much-needed new aircraft designs arrived in service from October 1944, by which time the Allies were on the offensive, with landings in the Philippines presaging a period of 'island-hopping' that would take the war towards the Japanese home islands. Despite new equipment,

The Mitsubishi G3M bomber served the Imperial Japanese Navy well during the 1930s, but it was rendered obsolete by mid-1942.

the IJA and IJN were now badly outnumbered and increasingly outclassed in terms of both available aircraft and pilots. After the successive fall of the Marianas, the Philippines, Iwo Jima and Okinawa, it was left to the US Army Air Force's B-29 Superfortress heavy bombers to take the battle to the Japanese mainland.

Regular heavy bombing raids against the home islands began in June 1944, and forced the IJA and IJN on to the defensive. All too often, the fighters pressed into homeland defence duties lacked the performance to reach the high-flying bombers. With Japan expecting an invasion of the mainland, air operations began to be limited in an effort to preserve aircraft, fuel and pilots. In the event, the atomic bombs dropped on Hiroshima and Nagasaki in August 1945 served to bring the Pacific War to an end, but not before aircraft and aircrew of the IJA and IJN had been sacrificed in kamikaze attacks on the Allies in a desperate bid to turn the tide of a war that was already lost.

LAND-BASED BOMBERS AND RECONNAISSANCE AIRCRAFT

Soon after successfully waging wars with China in the early 1930s, which left Tokyo controlling a puppet state in Manchuria, the Imperial Japanese Army set about a wide-ranging overhaul of its air arm, which saw both an expansion in the size of the force and the introduction of new aircraft.

This chapter includes the following aircraft:
- Mitsubishi G3M 'Nell' and 'Tina'
- Mitsubishi Ki-15 and C5M 'Babs'
- Mitsubishi Ki-21 'Sally'
- Mitsubishi Ki-30 'Ann'
- Mitsubishi Ki-51 'Sonya'
- Kawasaki Ki-48 'Lily'
- Nakajima Ki-49 *Donryu* 'Helen'
- Mitsubishi Ki-46 'Dinah'
- Mitsubishi G4M 'Betty'
- Mitsubishi Ki-67 *Hiryu* 'Peggy'

A Mitsubishi G3M 'Nell', registration M-372, of the Imperial Japanese
Army Air Service, 1942.

9

Mitsubishi G3M 'Nell' and 'Tina'

Renowned for its ship-killing exploits in the early days of the conflict in the Pacific, the G3M was typical of the bomber-transports developed between the wars. For its time, it was one of the longest-ranged twin-engined medium bombers in the world.

The aircraft that began life in 1934 with the Kawasaki in-house designation of Ka-15 was tailored to meet a

---

G3M1

Weight Loaded: 7642kg (16,848lb)

Dimensions Length: 16.45m (53ft 11.75in), Wingspan: 25.00m (82ft 0.25in), Height: 3.69m (12ft 1.25in)

Powerplant Two 679kW (910hp) Mitsubishi Kinsei 3 radial piston engines

Speed 348km/h (216mph) at 2000m (6560ft)

Range unavailable

Ceiling 7480m (24,540ft)

Armament 3 x 7.7mm (0.303in) machine guns plus one 800kg (1764lb) torpedo or equivalent bombload

---

requirement for a twin-engined, land-based naval bomber and transport. The forward-thinking 9-Shi specification was the brainchild of Admiral Isoroku Yamamoto, who was a proponent of long-range, land-based naval air power for use in an offensive capacity.

The resulting aircraft employed a cantilever mid-wing monoplane configuration with retractable tailwheel undercarriage. The initial aircraft was powered by a pair of 559kW (750hp) Hiro Type 91 liquid-cooled engines. Although a rival existed to the Ka-15 in the form of the Nakajima LB-2, the earlier success of the Ka-9 long-range reconnaissance aircraft prototype

ensured that Mitsubishi would always be the victor in the race to fulfil the 9-Shi requirement.

Initial prototype

Under the power of the aforementioned Hiro engines, the first prototype Ka-15 took to the air in July 1935. The total prototype production run extended to no fewer than 20 aircraft, which were used to test a range of different engine and propeller combinations. Among the different engines tested were the Mitsubishi Kinsei 2 and 3 radials, while

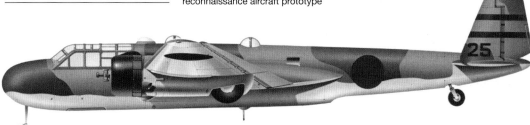

G3M1

Operated by the Kisarazu Kokutai at Omura on the island of Kyushu in August 1937, this aircraft flew raids on the Chinese towns of Nanking and Suzhou.

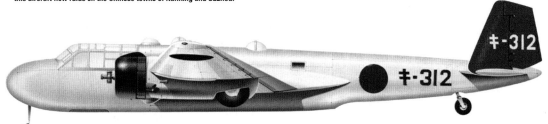

G3M1

Another Kisarazu Kokutai machine, this aircraft is seen as it appeared in April 1937. These were flown from Cheju Island for attacks against Chinese mainland targets in August 1937.

aircrews were sourced from both Japan and the United States. A total of six different configurations were tested, in the process of which the second prototype was lost in an accident.

Service trials were completed successfully, leading to an order under the formal designation Navy Type 96 Attack Bomber Model 11, otherwise known as the Mitsubishi G3M1.

The first 34 production aircraft, completed to G3M1 standard, were powered by 679kW (910hp) Mitsubishi Kinsei 3 engines. While the G3M1 was able to meet the original requirement of the Imperial Japanese Navy, its service use was limited by the fact that a successor was waiting in the wings.

This was the next major production derivative, the G3M2 Model 21, in which the Kinsei 3 engines were replaced by 802kW (1075hp) Kinsei 41 or 42 radials. The G3M2 also introduced increased fuel capacity, but the defensive armament was unchanged from the G3M1: three 7.7mm (0.303in) machine guns only, carried in each of the two retractable

G3M2 Model 22

Weight Maximum take-off: 8010kg (17,659lb)
Dimensions Length: 16.45m (53ft 11.75in), Wingspan: 25.00m (82ft 0.25in), Height: 3.69m (12ft 1.25in)
Powerplant Two 802kW (1075hp) Mitsubishi Kinsei 45 radial piston engines
Speed 374km/h (232mph) at 4200m (13,780ft)
Range 4380km (2722 miles)
Ceiling 9130m (29,954ft)
Armament 3 x 7.7mm (0.303in) machine guns, 1 x 20mm cannon plus one 800kg (1764lb) torpedo or equivalent bombload

G3M2
Three views depicting an aircraft of the 2nd Chutai, Genzan Kokutai, stationed in Saigon, Indo-China, in December 1941.

G3M2

A G3M2 of the Takao Kokutai, 23rd
Koku Sentai, based at Takao, Taiwan,
in April 1941.

G3M2

Based in Saigon, Indo-China, in December 1941,
this aircraft of the Genzan Kokutai took part in the
sinking of HMS *Prince of Wales* and *Repulse.*

dorsal turrets and one retractable
ventral turret. Later production
Model 21s introduced a new
powerplant in the form of the Kinsei 45,
which offered superior performance at
higher altitudes.

Once the defensive armament of the
G3M2 had been revised, the aircraft
was designated G3M2 Model 22.
Drawing from experience gained in
the fighting against the Chinese, the
Model 22 saw the dorsal and ventral
turrets removed and a large turret
housing a 20mm cannon was mounted
above the rear fuselage. A blister-type
position, each with a single 7.7mm
machine gun, was added on each side
of the rear fuselage. The dorsal turret,
with one 7.7mm gun, was retained, and
towards the end of the production run
the aircraft also began to sport a fourth
7.7mm weapon fired from the windows
of the cockpit.

With the G3M3 Model 23, the
engines were further uprated to the
Kinsei 51, now with an output of 969kW
(1300hp) each. Produced exclusively
by Nakajima, since Mitsubishi was now
concentrating on the G4M twin-engine,
land-based bomber, the G3M3 was the
fastest of all production versions, and
had its internal fuel capacity increased
to 5182 litres (1140 Imp gal), permitting
very long-range sorties up to a range of
6230km (3871 miles).

Transport versions

Transport had been one of the original
roles intended for the aircraft, and a
specialist version to fulfil this role was
the G3M1-L, a number of examples
being from the initial-production
G3M1. Another transport version of
the G3M1 was the L3Y1 Model 11 (or
Navy Type 96 Transport), its revised
designation originating from the

fact that aircraft conversions were
undertaken by the 1st Naval Air Arsenal
at Kasumigaura.

Once the improved G3M2 began
to be used as the basis for transport

'NAVAL BATTLE OFF MALAYA'
The G3M was one of two bomber
types involved in the Imperial
Japanese Navy's sinking of the
British battleship HMS *Prince of
Wales* and the battlecruiser HMS
Repulse, resulting in the loss of 840
sailors killed on 10 December 1941.
For this mission, a total of 60 G3M2s
operated by the Genzan and
Mihoro Kokutais joined forces with
26 Mitsubishi G4M1s, targeting the
Royal Navy vessels off the east coast
of Malaya near Kuantan, where they
were operating without air cover and
under radio silence. In Japanese,
the engagement is referred to as the
'Naval Battle off Malaya'.

derivatives, the result comprised the L3Y2 Model 12, which featured Kinsei 45 engines and defensive armament of a single 7.7mm machine gun. Both transport versions received the Allied reporting name 'Tina' to differentiate them from the bomber versions, which were known as 'Nell'.

The combat service of the G3M began with a long-range attack against Chinese targets in August 1937,

when a squadron of G3M2s flew from Taipei, Taiwan, to strike objectives in the Hangchow and Kwangteh areas, located 2010km (1249 miles) distant. The feat marked the first successful trans-oceanic bombing raid in history.

Pacific War honours

In World War II, the G3M made a name for itself with involvement in the raids against the British battleship HMS

Prince of Wales and the battlecruiser HMS *Repulse* in December 1941, only three days after the attack on Pearl Harbor had launched the war in the Pacific. Prior to the sinking of these warships, the G3M had also been involved in combat operations against US naval forces at Wake Island, and early actions also saw them take part in fighting in the Philippines and Marianas.

The G3M had begun to suffer at the hands of fighters as early as the Second Sino-Japanese War, and its survivability continued to deteriorate up until 1943, by which time most survivors had been withdrawn from front-line service and placed in secondary roles. These include glider-tug, bomber trainer and maritime reconnaissance, for which latter role it could be outfitted with search radar.

Total production figures for the 'Nell' and 'Tina' amounted to 1048 of all versions, of which Mitsubishi completed 636 with the remaining 412 built under sub-contract by Nakajima.

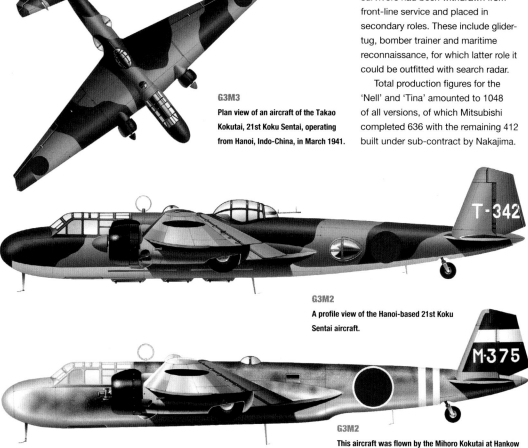

G3M3

Plan view of an aircraft of the Takao Kokutai, 21st Koku Sentai, operating from Hanoi, Indo-China, in March 1941.

G3M2

A profile view of the Hanoi-based 21st Koku Sentai aircraft.

G3M2

This aircraft was flown by the Mihoro Kokutai at Hankow for operations over China in May 1941.

Mitsubishi Ki-15 and C5M 'Babs'

A two-seat reconnaissance aircraft that served with distinction during the Sino-Japanese War, the 'Babs' was progressively improved for Army and Navy service but had mostly disappeared from the front line by 1943, after which some were used in kamikaze attacks.

Designed to meet a 1935 requirement of the Imperial Japanese Army calling for a two-seat reconnaissance aircraft, the Mitsubishi Ki-15 was launched as a joint military and civilian project, with two prototypes being completed accordingly.

The initial military prototype took to the air for the first time in May 1936, and after successfully undergoing service trials the aircraft was ordered into quantity production as the Army Type 97 Command Reconnaissance

Ki-15-I

Weight Maximum take-off: 2300kg (5071lb)
Dimensions Length: 8.70m (28ft 6.5in), Wingspan: 12.00m (39ft 4.25in), Height: 3.35m (11ft)
Powerplant One 477kW (640hp) Nakajima Ha-8 radial piston engine
Speed 480km/h (298mph) at 4000m (13,125ft)
Range 2400km (1491 miles)
Ceiling 11,400m (37,400ft)
Armament 1 x 7.7mm (0.303in) machine gun

Aircraft Model 1, or Ki-15-I. While deliveries of the first examples of the aircraft to the Army commenced in May 1937, development of the civilian version continued with a first flight of the prototype, named Kamikaze (Divine Wind). A limited production run saw the civilian Karigane I (Wild Goose I) version being produced for civilian operators in Japan.

At war with China

The Ki-15-I saw its baptism of fire during Japan's brutal war with China, and when the aircraft first appeared in this conflict it proved to be almost immune to the Chinese fighters then fielded. The situation turned against the Ki-15-I once the Soviet-built Polikarpov I-16 fighter began to appear in Chinese hands.

In an effort to improve the performance of the basic aircraft the Ki-15-II was developed, this

introducing a 671kW (900hp) Mitsubishi Ha-26-I engine. It entered service in 1939. Another bid to improve performance resulted in the Ki-15-III, two prototypes being completed of this version, which was powered by a 783kW (1050hp) Mitsubishi 102 radial.

As well as seeing service with the Army, the Ki-15 was adopted by the Imperial Japanese Navy as the Navy Type 96 Reconnaissance Aircraft Model 1 (otherwise known as C5M2). A batch of 30 aircraft was completed for Navy service as the C5M2, this time powered by a 708kW (950hp) Nakajima Sakae 12 engine.

To the Allies the Ki-15 and C5M were known as 'Babs', and a total of 489 examples of all versions had been built when manufacture came to an end. By 1943, most surviving Ki-15 aircraft had been relegated to second-line duties.

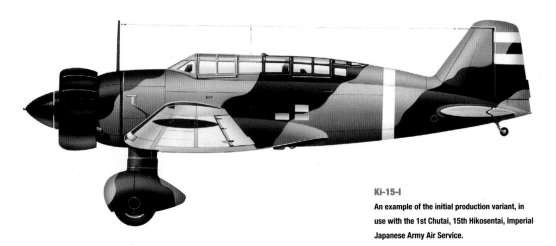

Ki-15-I

An example of the initial production variant, in use with the 1st Chutai, 15th Hikosentai, Imperial Japanese Army Air Service.

Mitsubishi Ki-21 'Sally'

At the time of its appearance, the Ki-21 helped bring the Imperial Japanese Army Air Service into the modern era, and although it was obsolescent by 1943 the aircraft remained popular with its crews and continued to serve until the end of the war.

In 1936 the Imperial Japanese Army issued a specification for a four-seat heavy bomber in order to replace the Army Type 92 Heavy Bomber (Mitsubishi Ki-20) and the Army Type 93 Heavy Bomber (Mitsubishi Ki-1).

Powered by two Mitsubishi Ha-6 radial engines, the initial two prototypes of the twin-engined bomber, the Mitsubishi Ki-21-I, demonstrated performance at least as good as contemporary bombers in the same class. In terms of design, the Ki-21 was

---

Ki-21-Ia

Weight Maximum take-off: 7916kg (17,452lb)

Dimensions Length: 16.00m (52ft 6in), Wingspan: 22.50m (73ft 9.75in), Height: 4.35m (14ft 3.5in)

Powerplant Two 634kW (850hp) Nakajima Ha-5 Kai radial piston engines

Speed 432km/h (268mph) at 4000m (13,125ft)

Range 2700km (1680 miles)

Ceiling 8600m (28,215ft)

Armament 3 x 7.7mm (0.303in) machine guns plus a bombload of up to 1000kg (2205lb)

---

an all-metal cantilever monoplane with wings mounted at the mid-fuselage position and with a glazed nose to accommodate a bomb-aimer. The second prototype differed from the first in having a defensive armament of three 7.7mm (0.303in) machine guns, adding an extra weapon in the ventral step, complementing the guns in the nose and dorsal position as found in the first aircraft. A third prototype followed, now powered by a pair of 634kW (850hp) Nakajima Ha-5 engines and with a re-profiled hemispherical nose and a redesigned rear fuselage. A revised vertical fin also ensured that directional stability was improved.

After seeing off competition from the rival Nakajima Ki-19 design, the Mitsubishi aircraft was ordered into production as the Army Type 97 Heavy Bomber Model 1A, otherwise known as the Ki-21-Ia. In this form, the aircraft entered service in summer 1938, with the first production deliveries following

a batch of five pre-series aircraft that had been completed to the same standard as the third prototype. The Ki-21-Ia was essentially similar to these, but introduced an increase in fuel capacity.

Operational experience

Once tested under combat conditions in China, it became apparent that the basic aircraft was lacking defensive armament. The result of these lessons was the Ki-21-Ib (Army Type 97 Heavy Bomber Model 1B), which increased the number of defensive machine guns from three to five through the addition of a single machine gun firing from lateral positions on either side of the rear fuselage, plus a remotely controlled weapon in a tail barbette.

Next in the line of bombers that would receive the Allied reporting name 'Sally' was the Ki-21-Ic (Army Type 97 Heavy Bomber Model 1C), which featured increased fuel capacity thanks

Ki-21-Ia

Wearing an overall olive green and brown upper-surface camouflage scheme, this Ki-21-Ia served with the 2nd Chutai, 60th Sentai, and operated over Manchuria in 1939.

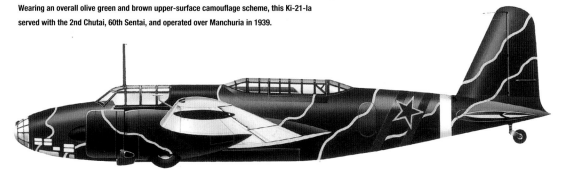

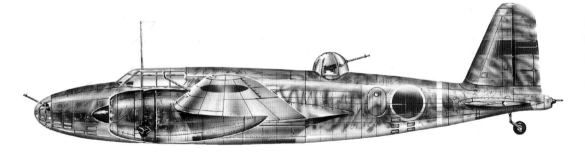

Ki-21-IIb

An anonymous Mitsubishi Ki-21-IIb as it
appeared in Imperial Japanese Army service
in 1944.

to an auxiliary fuel tank fitted in the
rear bomb-bay. Another change in the
defensive armament saw the addition
of one additional machine gun for a
total of two weapons located in lateral
positions.

With the next stage in the aircraft's
evolution, Mitsubishi introduced the
Ki-21-II, which in prototype form was
the first in the family to be powered by
the more powerful Mitsubishi Ha-101
engines, each of which developed
1119kW (1500hp). The new aircraft
resulted from the Army's aspiration
to field an improved version of the
bomber that would offer better speed
and ceiling figures when faced by
modern fighters in the upcoming Pacific
Campaign.

The initial production version of the
'second-generation' Ki-21-II was the
Ki-21-IIa, which entered production
with the same armament as the Ki-21-
Ic after completing flight trials in late
1940. Its full service designation was
Army Type 97 Heavy Bomber Model 2A.
By the start of the Pacific War, the Ki-
21-IIa was the standard bomber among
Army heavy bomber groups.

The final version to enter quantity
production was the Ki-21-IIb (Army
Type 97 Heavy Bomber Model 2B),

with a number of refinements including
deletion of the dorsal 'greenhouse'
and its replacement with a turret for a
12.7mm (0.5in) machine gun (which led
to it briefly being assigned the reporting
name 'Gwen'). Late-production aircraft
also added individual exhaust stacks
for an increase in thrust.

As well as the aforementioned
military variants of the 'Sally', the
aircraft was adapted for transport use,
using surplus Ki-21-Ia airframes.

The final production figures for the
Ki-21 amounted to 2064 aircraft built,
of which 1713 were by Mitsubishi and
351 were by Nakajima.

'Sally' at war

In the first stages of the Pacific War, the
Ki-21 continued to play an important
role among the Army's bomber units.
Despite its increasing vulnerability
to the Allied fighters in theatre, the

Ki-21-IIb

Weight Maximum take-off: 10,610kg (23,391lb)

Dimensions Length: 16.00m (52ft 6in), Wingspan:
22.50m (73ft 9.75in), Height: 4.85m (15ft 11in)

Powerplant Two 1119kW (1500hp) Mitsubishi
Ha-101 radial piston engines

Speed 485km/h (301mph) at 4720m (15,485ft)

Range 2700km (1678 miles)

Ceiling 10,000m (32,810ft)

Armament 5 x 7.7mm (0.303in) machine guns,
1 x 12.7mm (0.5in) machine gun plus a bombload
of up to 1000kg (2205lb)

now-antiquated bomber could still be
found in front-line units at the time of
the Japanese surrender. Indeed, thanks
to its excellent handling and ease of
maintenance it was sometimes preferred
to the more modern Ki-49.

Despite its obsolescence, the Ki-21 'Sally'
remained a front-line aircraft until the end of
the war.

Mitsubishi Ki-30 'Ann'

A stalwart of the campaign fought in China, the Ki-30 was a highly conventional light bomber that saw out its service during the Pacific War, in which it was soon demoted to second-line duties after being confronted by modern Allied fighter opposition.

The Mitsubishi Ki-30 was designed to meet an Imperial Japanese Army specification of May 1936 outlining a light bomber in order to replace the Kawasaki Ki-3 and Mitsubishi Ki-2.

A prototype of the Ki-30 was first flown in February 1937, with the initial powerplant of a 615kW (825hp) Mitsubishi Ha-6 air-cooled engine. Innovations included an internal bomb-bay, variable-pitch propeller and – in a first for a Japanese light bomber – a double-row radial engine. Retractable undercarriage was originally included in the design, but this gave way to fixed, spatted landing gear once construction began.

The second prototype appeared soon after, now re-engined with a more powerful Nakajima Ha-5 Kai engine. As well as offering superior performance over the initial prototype, the second aircraft also exceeded all the performance requirements laid

out in the Army's specification. On the basis of this success, Mitsubishi was contracted to produce a batch of 20 aircraft for service trials, and these were delivered in early 1938. After service trials with the pre-production batch, the Ki-30 was ordered into quantity production in March 1938, under the official designation Army Type 97 Light Bomber.

Losses mount

The Ki-30 saw its combat debut in the war with China, and achieved good results when it was provided with fighter escort, typically in the shape of the Ki-27. After the attack on Pearl Harbor, the aircraft saw action over the Philippines once the Japanese had gained air superiority there. However, when Allied fighters began to take the initiative during the Pacific War, the aircraft that received the Allied reporting name 'Ann' was found wanting and

began to be relegated to less important theatres of action. In common with many other types of aircraft that were withdrawn from front-line use, examples of the Ki-30 were used for devastating kamikaze missions at the close of the war.

In total, 704 examples of the Ki-30 were manufactured, of which 68 were completed by the 1st Army Air Arsenal at Tachikawa.

Ki-30

Weight Maximum take-off: 3220kg (7099lb)
Dimensions Length: 10.35m (33ft 11.5in), Wingspan: 14.55m (47ft 8.75in), Height: 3.65m (11ft 11.75in)
Powerplant One 708kW (950hp) Nakajima Ha-5 Kai radial piston engine
Speed 425km/h (264mph) at 4000m (13,125ft)
Range 1700km (1056 miles)
Ceiling 8570m (28,115ft)
Armament 2 x 7.7mm (0.303in) machine guns plus a bombload of up to 400kg (882lb)

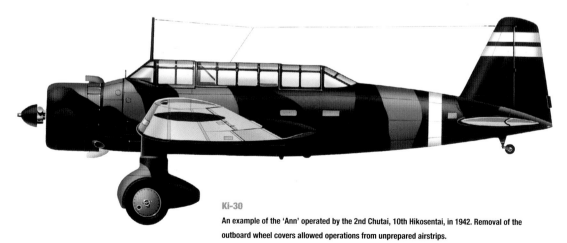

Ki-30

An example of the 'Ann' operated by the 2nd Chutai, 10th Hikosentai, in 1942. Removal of the outboard wheel covers allowed operations from unprepared airstrips.

Mitsubishi Ki-51 'Sonya'

A standard ground-attack aircraft of the Imperial Japanese Army throughout the Pacific War, the Ki-51 was agile, well protected and simple to both fly and maintain. However, its relatively low speed meant that it soon became easy prey for Allied fighter aircraft.

Developed on the basis of the Ki-30, the Ki-51 was intended as a ground-attack aircraft that would emphasize manoeuvrability, protection and the ability to operate from forward airstrips close to the battle. At the same time it was to be smaller than its predecessor.

The Imperial Japanese Army specification of 1937 that led to the Ki-51 saw construction of two prototypes by Mitsubishi, these being powered by the same company's Ha-26-II

Ki-51 (late production)
Weight Maximum take-off: 2920kg (6437lb)
Dimensions Length: 9.20m (30ft 2.25in), Wingspan: 12.10m (39ft 8.25in), Height: 2.73m (8ft 11.5in)
Powerplant One 701kW (940hp) Mitsubishi Ha-26-II radial piston engine
Speed 425km/h (264mph) at 3000m (9845ft)
Range 1060km (659 miles)
Ceiling 8270m (27,130ft)
Armament 1 x 7.7mm (0.303in) machine gun, 2 x 12.7mm (0.5in) machine guns plus a bombload of up to 200kg (441lb)

engine. Both aircraft were flight-tested beginning in summer 1939.

While reduced in size compared to the Ki-30, the Ki-51 employed the same basic configuration, although the bomb-bay was deleted, meaning that the wing could not be set lower on the fuselage. Other changes addressed the cockpit, which continued to accommodate a crew of two.

Service trials
After the prototypes, Mitsubishi completed a batch of 11 aircraft for service trials. These differed in items of equipment including armour protection for the crew and engine, and aerodynamic improvements aimed at improving handling at low speed.

The production aircraft were built to the same standard as the service trials machines, under the designation Army Type 99 Assault Aircraft, later examples adding increased fuel capacity.

First employed in combat over China, the Ki-51 was used throughout

the war in the Pacific. However, the Ki-51 proved vulnerable to interception (in common with the Ki-30), which limited its efficiency in all but non-contested environments.

The impressive total production run eventually reached 2385 examples, built by both Mitsubishi (1472) and the 1st Army Air Arsenal (913).

Variants
The only major derivatives of the 'Sonya' were the Ki-51a, a one-off tactical reconnaissance prototype converted from a standard Ki-51 airframe; and the Ki-71, a further development of the aircraft similarly intended for a reconnaissance role.

The Ki-71, of which three prototypes were completed, was powered by a 1119kW (1500hp) Mitsubishi Ha-112-II engine and featured the retractable landing gear that had originally been envisaged for the Ki-51. Neither of these reconnaissance versions entered production.

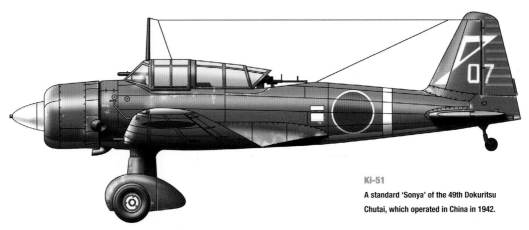

Ki-51

A standard 'Sonya' of the 49th Dokuritsu Chutai, which operated in China in 1942.

Kawasaki Ki-48 'Lily'

A twin-engined light bomber, the Ki-48 was schemed as a Japanese counterpart to the influential Soviet-built Tupolev SB Fast Bomber. Although it eventually proved vulnerable to fighter interception, its production and development continued until late 1944.

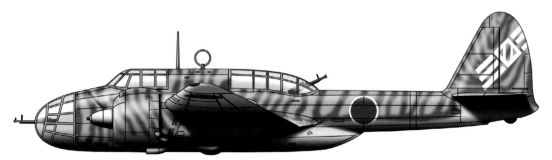

In 1937 the Imperial Japanese Army issued a requirement for a high-performance twin-engined light bomber, and Kawasaki was instructed to design and develop the aircraft, which emerged as the Ki-48.

In terms of layout, the Ki-48 prototype was a cantilever mid-wing monoplane with retractable landing gear and a crew of four. The fuselage accommodated a bomb-bay, and power was provided by a pair of 708kW (950hp) Nakajima Ha-25 radial engines.

The first prototype took to the air in July 1939 and was followed by three more examples and five pre-production machines. These were used to iron out various teething troubles before

the aircraft was ready to be launched into production as the Army Type 99 Twin-Engine Light Bomber Model 1A, or Ki-48-Ia. Minor equipment changes produced the Ki-48-Ib, which added improved defensive gun mountings.

Improved version

While the performance of the initial production version was adequate when operated under combat conditions in China beginning in autumn 1940, by the time the Pacific War was in full swing it was found that the Ki-48-Ia was too slow and poorly armed to fight off Allied opposition.

As a result, development work proceeded on an improved Ki-48-II, which was powered by Nakajima Ha-115 engines and added armour protection for the crew and the fuel tanks. After testing of the prototype Ki-48-II, three of which were completed, this version entered production in spring 1942 as the Army Type 99 Twin-Engine Light Bomber Model 2A, or Ki-48-IIa.

While the defensive armament of the Ki-48-IIa actually remained unchanged from that of the Ki-48-Ia, the maximum bombload was increased to 800kg

Ki-48-Ib

This aircraft was operated by the 1st Chutai, 34th Sentai, based in Thailand in April 1943. The inadequate combat performance of the Ki-48-I spurred development of the much-improved Ki-48-II in 1942.

(1764lb). The Ki-48-IIb was the next production version, generally similar to the Ki-48-IIa but with dive brakes fitted on the undersides of each outer wing panel. The Ki-48-IIc finally addressed the defensive armament, adding an additional 12.7mm (0.5in) machine gun.

Total production of all versions of the Ki-48 amounted to 1977.

Ki-48-IIb

Weight Maximum take-off: 6750kg (14,881lb)
Dimensions Length: 12.75m (41ft 10in), Wingspan: 17.45m (57ft 3in), Height: 3.80m (12ft 5.5in)
Powerplant Two 858kW (1150hp) Nakajima Ha-115 radial piston engines
Speed 505km/h (314mph) maximum
Range 2400km (1491 miles)
Ceiling 10,100m (33,135ft)
Armament 3 x 7.7mm (0.303in) machine guns, plus a maximum bombload of 800kg (1764lb), or a normal bombload of 400kg (882lb)

Ki-48 TEST-BEDS
The Ki-48 proved to be an adaptable platform and found use as a test-bed for a variety of experimental projects. In 1944, the aircraft was adapted for trials of a new air-to-ground guided missile, the I-Go-1-B. A total of four Ki-48-IIbs were eventually modified for launch of the missile. Meanwhile, another Ki-48-IIb served as a flying test-bed for the Ne-0, an experimental jet engine. For this installation, the bomb-bay doors were removed and the engine was slung under the fuselage.

Nakajima Ki-49 *Donryu* 'Helen'

Nakajima's *Donryu* (Storm Dragon) was the result of an ambitious programme to develop a heavy bomber that could operate without fighter escort, using speed and defensive armament for survival. In the event, the production Ki-49 was found somewhat wanting.

Planned as the ultimate successor to the Mitsubishi Ki-21 (Army Type 97 Heavy Bomber), which had entered service in 1938, the Nakajima Ki-49, while classed as a heavy bomber, was more comparable with a Western medium bomber. As schemed, the new bomber was intended to have sufficient speed and defensive armament to survive in combat without close fighter escort.

After Nakajima's Ki-19 had lost out to the rival Mitsubishi Ki-21 in its bid to fulfil a 1937 specification for a heavy

bomber, the losing manufacturer had been awarded a production contract to manufacture the Ki-21. This provided useful experience in the design of a new bomber, the Ki-49, which was drafted by a design team led by Nishimura, Itokawa and, as project leader, T. Koyama.

First prototype

The Nakajima design that was drafted to meet the Imperial Japanese Army's aforementioned specification of early 1938 was a cantilever mid-wing monoplane powered in its initial form by two 708kW (950hp) Nakajima Ha-5 Kai radial engines. Other specifics of the requirement included a maximum speed of 500km/h (311 mph), representing an increase of 16 per cent over the Ki-21, and a range of 3000km (1864 miles). The aircraft had internal accommodation for eight crew and a bomb-bay tailored to carry the maximum load of 1000kg (2205lb) as specified in the original requirement.

The initial prototype of the Ka-49 took to the air for the first time in

August 1939. Compared to the first prototype, the second and third aircraft were equipped with 932kW (1250hp) Nakajima Ha-41 engines. The same powerplant was retained by the seven pre-production aircraft.

In its prototype configuration, the Ki-49's defensive armament consisted of five 7.7mm (0.303in) machine guns, of which the tail installation represented the first time that an Imperial Japanese Army bomber had been equipped with a tail turret. These weapons were complemented by a single flexible 20mm cannon in the port side of a dorsal turret.

Other key features of the Ki-49 prototype included Fowler-type flaps extending from the wing root to the ailerons in order to improve take-off and climb performance. Self-protection features included self-sealing fuel tanks, six of which were carried in the wing centre-section, and two in each outer-wing panel.

Ki-49-I

Weight Maximum take-off: 10,675kg (23,534lb)

Dimensions Length: 16.80m (55ft 1.75in), Wingspan: 20.42m (67ft), Height: 4.25m (13ft 11.25in)

Powerplant Two 932kW (1250hp) Nakajima Ha-41 radial piston engines

Speed unavailable

Range unavailable

Ceiling unavailable

Armament 5 x 7.7mm (0.303in) machine guns, 1 x 20mm cannon plus a maximum bombload of 1000kg (2205lb)

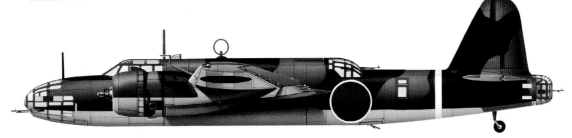

Ki-49-I

A Ki-49-I as it appeared during service in China in early 1944 wearing the 'segment-type' camouflage scheme.

After successful trials, the Ka-49 was ordered into production in March 1941 as the Army Type 100 Heavy Bomber Model I *Donryu*, otherwise known as the Ki-49-I. These aircraft were identical to the pre-series Ka-49 machines. Service entry was marked in August 1941 and the aircraft was initially deployed to China. However, once the war in the Pacific began the *Donryu* saw operational service around New Britain and New Guinea and also took part in attacks against mainland Australia.

Disappointing performance

Combat service revealed that the Ki-49-I was under-powered, and as a result longer-range missions could only be flown with a significantly reduced bombload. In practice, the Ki-49-I regularly operated with a bombload less than that carried by

the Ki-21. Another drawback was the aircraft's flying qualities, which service personnel judged inferior to those of its predecessor. In its favour, the Ki-49-I's defensive armament was found to be generally effective, and its self-sealing fuel tanks added to its survivability.

In an effort to address its deficiencies, Nakajima flew a re-engined version in spring 1942. This,

Above: A Ki-49 *Donryu* 'Helen' is strafed by an Allied fighter aircraft while on the ground.

the Ki-49-II, was powered by a pair of more powerful Nakajima Ha-109 (Army Type 2) engines driving constant-speed propellers. After two prototypes of this revised version, production was

Ki-49-I

In late 1943 this aircraft was serving in a training role with the Hamamatsu Army Flying School.

Ki-49-IIa

An aircraft of the 3rd Chutai, 61st Sentai, based in Taiwan in 1945. The stylized tail marking represents the number 61.

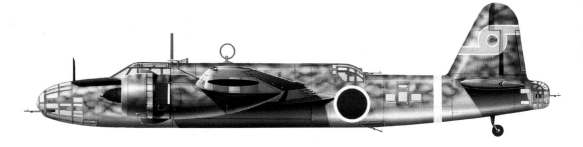

Ki-49-IIa

Based in the Dutch East Indies, this 3rd Chutai, 62nd Sentai, aircraft operated over Burma, the Dutch East Indies and New Guinea from January–October 1944.

launched as the Ki-49-IIa, or Army Type 100 Heavy Bomber Model 2A. Differences included further improved self-sealing tanks, a new bombsight and additional, more effective armour plating. Deliveries to Army units commenced in August 1942.

While the Ki-49-IIa retained the defensive armament of the original Ki-49-I, the improved Ki-49-IIb introduced revised armament. The initial defensive armament (Ki-49-I and Ki-49-IIa) had comprised single flexible 7.7mm

Ki-58 ESCORT FIGHTER
While successive variants of the Ki-49 added heavier defensive armament in an effort to stave off the attentions of Allied fighters, a more radical approach to the problem of interception by the enemy was embodied in the Ki-58, of which three prototypes were constructed between late 1940 and spring 1941. This aircraft was intended as an escort fighter that could accompany standard bombers all the way to their targets, and had its bomb-bay replaced by a ventral gondola and an armament of five 20mm cannon and three 7.7mm (0.303in) machine guns. It did not see combat service.

(0.303in) machine guns in each of the nose, ventral, port and starboard beam and tail positions, plus a 20mm cannon in the dorsal turret. In contrast, the Ki-49-IIb introduced three new 12.7mm weapons, replacing the previous three 7.7mm calibre weapons in the nose, ventral and tail positions. The 20mm dorsal gun and the two 7.7mm beam guns were retained. The heavier-calibre weapons were intended to provide greater destructive power when tackling enemy interceptors, which frequently survived damage inflicted by the 7.7mm rifle-calibre guns.

Despite the Nakajima Ha-109 (Army Type 2) powerplant, the introduction of increasingly capable Allied fighters to the Pacific theatre meant that the performance of the *Donryu* still fell short in its improved Ki-49-II versions. Once in service, the Ki-49-IIs were assigned to Army units operating in New Guinea as well as in China. However, the new aircraft never completely replaced the earlier Ki-21-II.

New engines
The next major effort to overhaul the performance of the *Donryu* was the Ki-49-III, which introduced the Nakajima Ha-117 engines with an output of 1805kW (2240hp). At the time these engines were the most powerful 14-cylinder radial engines ever developed. Ultimately, it had been hoped that engine power output could

be increased to as much as 2088kW (2800hp). However, the engines never managed to overcome their reliability problems. As a result, and after the completion by Nakajima of six prototypes, the ultimate bomber version of the Ki-49, production of the *Donryu* was brought to an end in December 1944.

Without the improvement in performance that was required to remain relevant as a heavy bomber in the Pacific campaign, the *Donryu* began to be shifted to other, less critical combat roles, although development of additional variants continued. Typical roles for the aircraft towards the end of the war included anti-submarine patrol, troop transport and, finally, kamikaze attack aircraft. For the anti-submarine role, the *Donryu* could be outfitted with electronic and magnetic detection equipment.

The *Donryu*'s useful load-carrying capacity rendered it an effective kamikaze raider. For this role the aircraft were typically operated by a crew of two, with all defensive armament removed. In this configuration, the aircraft could be packed with up to 1600kg (3527lb) of bombs.

More unusual was the adaptation of the *Donryu* as a night-fighter. In this capacity, the aircraft was operated as a 'hunter-killer' team, with one aircraft fitted with a searchlight to illuminate enemy aircraft and the other mounting a 75mm cannon in the fuselage. However, the concept was not a success due to the poor performance of the modified aircraft.

Fighting Storm Dragon

Typical of the *Donryu*'s later-war fortunes were the actions near the Philippines once the Allies had returned to this theatre of action. Here, the bomber suffered badly at the hands of enemy fighters, and, from late 1944, they were transferred to units that undertook kamikaze suicide attacks against the Allied fleet involved in landings at Mindoro.

Above all, while the *Donryu* had proven itself a better-protected bomber than any other Japanese equipment (at least until the arrival of the superior

Ki-67), the aircraft was always hampered by its poor performance. In particular, speed at low and medium altitudes was deemed unsatisfactory, and the Ki-21 remained better regarded as a 'pilot's aircraft'. Ironically, the early design of the *Donryu*, with its mid-mounted, low-aspect-ratio wing, had been expected to ensure good handling at exactly these altitudes.

Total production of the *Donryu* amounted to 819 aircraft, comprising 769 built by the parent company, and 50 more manufactured by Tachikawa.

The Nakajima production run included three examples of the Ki-58 (see boxed item) as well as two prototypes of the Ki-80. The latter was intended to serve as a pathfinder for bomber formations. After the pathfinder

version was abandoned, the prototype Ki-80s were instead used for tests of the Nakajima Ha-117 engine.

The Allied reporting name 'Helen' was applied to all variants.

Ki-49-IIa

Weight Maximum take-off: 11,400kg (25,133lb)
Dimensions Length: 16.50m (54ft 1.5in), Wingspan: 20.42m (67ft), Height: 4.25m (13ft 11.25in)
Powerplant Two 1119kW (1500hp) Nakajima Ha-109 radial piston engines
Speed 492km/h (306mph) at 5000m (16,405ft)
Range 2950km (1833 miles)
Ceiling 9300m (30,150ft)
Armament 5 x 7.7mm (0.303in) machine guns, 1 x 20mm cannon plus a maximum bombload of 1000kg (2205lb)

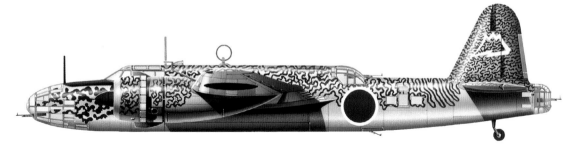

Ki-49-IIa

A disruptive 'snake-weave' camouflage pattern on an aircraft of the 1st Chutai, 7th Sentai, in 1943.

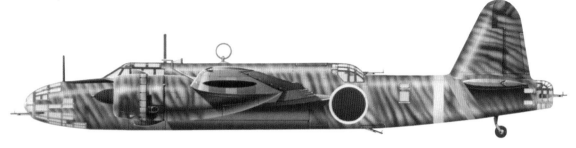

Ki-49-IIa

Stationed in north-east China in September 1944, this *Donryu* was flown by the 3rd Chutai, 95th Sentai, wearing 'palm-frond' camouflage.

Mitsubishi Ki-46 'Dinah'

Originating as a high-altitude reconnaissance aircraft, the sleek Ki-46 eventually saw service as an interceptor and ground-attack fighter, too. In its original role, the 'Dinah' remained one of the most impressive aircraft to see service during World War II.

In 1937, the Imperial Japanese Army announced a requirement for a high-performance reconnaissance aircraft in order to replace the Ki-15, and Mitsubishi responded with its Ki-46 design. Among the sleekest aircraft fielded by any nation in World War II, the prototype Ki-46 as first flown in November 1939 was a two-seat cantilever low-wing monoplane, powered by a pair of 671kW (900hp) Mitsubishi Ha-21-I radial engines. The undercarriage was fully retractable and of the tailwheel type.

During initial flight-testing, it was discovered that the top speed of the Ki-46 was somewhat lower than demanded by the specification. However, overall performance was still better than any comparable aircraft in service with the Imperial Japanese Army or Navy, and as a result the aircraft was ordered into production as the Army Type 100 Command Reconnaissance Aircraft Model I, or the Ki-61-I.

In its early period of operational service the Ki-46-I exhibited a number

of shortcomings, resulting in the development of the Ki-46-II powered by 805kW (1080hp) Mitsubishi Ha-102 engines. Thus equipped, the aircraft now possessed a maximum speed in excess of that outlined by the original specification. Ultimately, the Ki-46-II became the most important production version of the aircraft that received the Allied reporting name 'Dinah', with a total of over 1000 examples built. Of these, a number were later converted to become three-seat radio/navigation trainers as the Ki-46-II Kai.

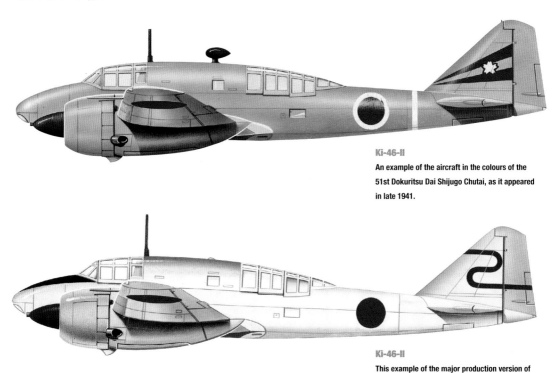

Ki-46-II

An example of the aircraft in the colours of the 51st Dokuritsu Dai Shijugo Chutai, as it appeared in late 1941.

Ki-46-II

This example of the major production version of the 'Dinah' served with the 76th Dokuritsu Hiko Chutai based in the East Indies in 1943.

Ki-46-III Kai

Armed with twin 20mm Ho-5 nose cannon, and an oblique forward-firing 37mm Ho-203 cannon, this Ki-46-III Kai was flown by the 17th Dokuritsu Hiko Chutai.

Offering even greater speed was the Ki-46-III, of which 609 were completed. Some of these were in turn converted to become interceptors under the Ki-46-III Kai designation, or as ground-attack aircraft under the designation Ki-46-IIIb.

At the end of the war, testing of a further improved Ki-46-IV – powered by 1119kW (1500hp) Mitsubishi Ha-112-II Ru turbocharged engines for enhanced high-altitude performance – was still under way.

In combat

The 'Dinah' saw service throughout the duration of the Pacific War, and although it remained a useful asset for the Army, losses began to mount once more capable Allied fighters started to appear in numbers. This was the case for the Ki-46-II, at least, although it should be noted that the higher-performing Ki-46-III remained almost immune to fighter interception until the end of the war. Production of all models eventually amounted to 1742 aircraft.

Ki-46-III Kai

Weight Maximum take-off: 3830kg (8444lb)

Dimensions Length: 11.00m (36ft 1in), Wingspan: 14.70m (48ft 2.75in), Height: 3.88m (12ft 8.75in)

Powerplant Two 1119kW (1500hp) Mitsubishi Ha-112-II radial piston engines

Speed 630km/h (391mph) at 6000m (19,685ft)

Range 4000km (2485 miles)

Ceiling 10,500m (34,450ft)

Armament 2 x 20mm cannon and 1 x 37mm oblique cannon

Mitsubishi G4M 'Betty'

The most prolific Japanese bomber of the war, and also the most famous, the Navy's G4M saw action across the Pacific theatre, beginning with impressive long-range actions against Allied outposts and ending with a defensive war to which it was not best suited.

In 1937, the Imperial Japanese Navy issued a 12-Shi specification for a land-based Attack Bomber that would succeed the G3M. The resulting aircraft was the Mitsubishi G4M, the prototype of which took to the air for the first time in October 1939. The aircraft's design allied a capacious fuselage with a mid-wing monoplane planform, while power was provided by a pair of 1141kW (1530hp) Mitsubishi Kasei 11 radial engines. Although the specification called for very long range, the design would forever be limited by the fact that it was powered by only two rather than four engines.

After successfully completing service trials, the G4M was approved for production in 1940 as the Navy Type 1 Attack Bomber Model 11, otherwise known as the G4M1 Model 1. This aircraft represented the first series-production version, and it began to be issued to front-line units in the summer of 1941. It was the G4M1 that brought lasting fame to the aircraft when examples were involved in the sinking of the British battleship HMS *Prince of Wales* and the battlecruiser HMS *Repulse* in December 1940. The same variant was used for the raids against Darwin in Australia in February 1942. Less auspiciously, it was a pair of G4M1s carrying Admiral Isoroku Yamamoto that were shot down by US fighters over Bougainville in April 1943, robbing the Japanese of one of their finest tacticians. Compared to its G3M predecessor, however, the

The distinctive appearance of the G4M led to it receiving the name 'flying lighter' from those pilots that faced it. 'Hamaki', or 'flying cigar', was another name bestowed upon it by the Japanese.

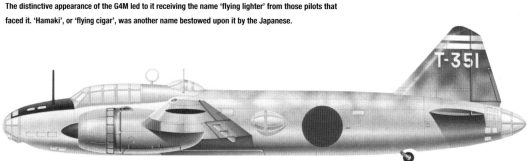

G4M1 Model 11

Flown by the Tatao Kokutai (later the 753rd Kokutai), this aircraft was based at Rabaul and involved in the fighting around New Guinea in October 1942.

G4M1 Model 11

Operated by the 705th Kokutai, this 'Betty' was based at Rabaul, New Britain, in 1943.

G4M1 Model 11

An example of the aircraft flown by the 761st
Kokutai from Kanoya in southern Kyushu in 1943.
The overall forest green colours are unusual for
the type.

G4M was notably better provided with
defensive armament. In the form of the
G4M1, this comprised single 7.7mm
(0.303in) machine guns in the nose and
dorsal blister, two similar weapons in
the beam positions and a single 20mm
cannon in the tail turret.

While the next production version,
the G4M1 Model 12, was generally
similar to the Model 1 but was powered
by new Kasei 15 engines for improved
high-altitude performance, more
significant changes were embodied in
the G4M2 Model 22, which introduced

G4M1 Model 11

This early G4M1 served with the 1st Chutai of the
Takao Kokutai (later reconstituted as the 753rd
Kokutai) on the Rabaul front in September 1942.

another new powerplant in the shape
of 1342kW (1800hp) Mitsubishi MK4P
Kasei 21 engines, and a number
of other improvements including a
laminar-flow wing, increased tailplane
area, rounded wing and tail tips,
increased nose glazing and additional
defensive armament. The G4M2
Model 22A and G4M2 Model 22B were
basically similar to the G4M2, but with
changes to their defensive armament
configurations.

Last of the line

Another new powerplant was
introduced in the G4M2a Model 24,
powered by a pair of 1361kW (1825hp)
MK4T Kasei 25 engines. This variant
also added bulged bomb-bay doors.
The G4M2a Model 24A, 24B and
24C, meanwhile, featured successive
armament changes; late-production
aircraft also had an air-surface radar.

The last production version of
the aircraft codenamed 'Betty' by

the Allies was the G4M3 Model 34,
which attempted to rectify the various
shortcomings of its predecessors.
As such, this version incorporated
self-sealing fuel tanks and more
extensive armour protection. The G4M3
arrived too late in the war to make
any meaningful impression, and only
60 examples were ever completed. It is
very likely that, had adequate armour

G4M1 Model 11

Weight Loaded: 9500kg (20,944b)
Dimensions Length: 20.00m (65ft 7.5in),
Wingspan: 25.00m (82ft 0.25in), Height: 6.00m
(19ft 8.25in)
Powerplant Two 1141kW (1530hp) Mitsubishi
MK4A Kasei 11 radial piston engines
Speed 428km/h (266mph) at 4200m (13,780ft)
Range 6033km (3749 miles)
Ceiling unavailable
Armament 4 x 7.7mm (0.303in) machine guns,
1 x 20mm cannon plus a maximum bombload of
1000kg (2205lb)

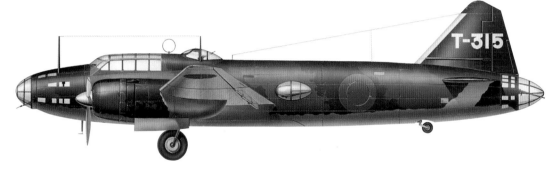

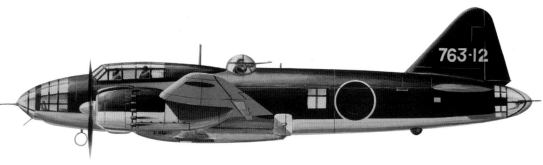

G4M2 Model 22

Weight Loaded: 12,500kg (27,558lb)
Dimensions Length: 20.00m (65ft 7.5in),
Wingspan: 25.00m (82ft 0.25in), Height: 6.00m
(19ft 8.25in)
Powerplant Two 1342kW (1800hp) Mitsubishi
MK4P Kasei 21 radial piston engines
Speed 438km/h (272mph) at 4600m (15,090ft)
Range 6059km (3765 miles)
Ceiling 8950m (29,365ft)
Armament 4 x 7.7mm (0.303in) machine guns,
2 x 20mm cannon plus a maximum bombload of
1000kg (2205lb)

protection and self-sealing tanks been
introduced to the aircraft at an earlier
date, then the bomber's success would
have been much improved.

A number of experimental versions
were completed to test alternative
powerplants. These included one
G4M2B Model 25, two G4M2c
Model 26, one G4M2d Model 27 and
two G4M3 Model 36 aircraft.

G4M3 Model 34

Based at Atsugi at the end of the war, this is an
example of the final production model of the
'Betty', and was flown by the Yokosuka Kokutai.

As Japan's fortunes in the war took
a turn for the worse, the G4M was
adopted as the carrier aircraft for the
Navy's MXY7 *Ohka* (Cherry Blossom)
piloted missile used for suicide attacks.
Aircraft equipped for the carriage and
launch of this weapon were designated
G4M2e Model 24J, and replaced the
bomb-bay doors with shackles.

Another specialist adaptation of the
'Betty' was the G6M1, or Navy Type 1
Wingtip Convoy Fighter, intended
as a long-range escort fighter for
service in the Sino-Japanese War, and
equipped for the purpose with heavier
defensive armament in the form of four
20mm cannon and a single 7.7mm
machine gun. Although the G6M1
concept proved unsuccessful, some
of the 30 examples completed were
subsequently adapted as transports
as the G6M1-L2, which served
on paratrooper duties during the
Pacific War, or as trainers under the
designation G6M1-K.

By the time production of Japan's
most prolific bomber had come to
an end, a total of 2446 of all versions
of the 'Betty' had been completed,

G4M2a Model 24A

Assigned to the 702nd Hikotai, 763rd Kokutai, and
shown carrying an Ohka missile, this aircraft was
camouflaged overall dark green and was captured
at Clark Field, Philippines, in 1944.

including prototypes and the G6M1s.

At the close of the war, a pair of
G4M1s was employed to transport the
Japanese surrender delegation to Ie-
Shima on 19 August 1945.

G4M3 Model 34

Weight Maximum take-off: 12,500kg (27,558lb)
Dimensions Length: 19.50m (63ft 11.75in),
Wingspan: 25.00m (82ft 0.25in), Height: 6.00m
(19ft 8.25in)
Powerplant Two 1361kW (1825hp) Mitsubishi
MK4T Kasei 25 radial piston engines
Speed 470km/h (292mph) at 5150m (16,895ft)
Range 4335km (2694 miles)
Ceiling 9220m (30,250ft)
Armament 2 x 7.7mm (0.303in) machine guns,
4 x 20mm cannon plus a maximum bombload of
1000kg (2205lb)

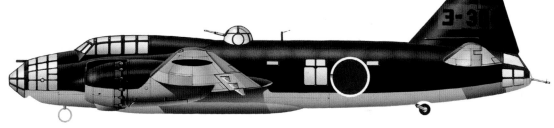

Mitsubishi Ki-67 *Hiryu* 'Peggy'

The finest Japanese bomber of World War II, the *Hiryu* (Flying Dragon) arrived too late in the conflict to fulfil its true potential. In the event, the aircraft was hopelessly outnumbered by Allied opposition and its crews were typically poorly trained for combat.

In early 1941, while the new Nakajima Ki-49 was undergoing service trials, the Imperial Japanese Army put out a call to Mitsubishi for the design and manufacture of three prototypes of a new tactical heavy bomber to meet a specification that it had drawn up. Long-term plans envisaged the new bomber being used in action against the Soviet Union.

The result was the Ki-67, a prototype of which was first flown in

December 1942. The aircraft was a cantilever mid-wing monoplane with a fuselage providing accommodation for a crew of between six and eight, and a large bomb-bay. In prototype form, the Ki-67 was powered by two Mitsubishi Ha-104 radial engines.

Ultimately, a total of 17 prototype and pre-production test aircraft were completed and these proved successful in trials, leading to the launch of quantity production under the designation Army Type 4 Heavy Bomber Model 1 *Hiryu*, or Ki-67-I, in December 1943.

Production model

While the Army had originally envisaged a series of different variants to fulfil different tasks, the precarious war situation meant the production concentrated on the Ki-67-I, assigned the Allied reporting name 'Peggy'.

After 160 of the initial production version had been completed, subsequent aircraft were equipped with torpedo racks. It was in the torpedo-

bomber role that the Ki-67 first went into combat, attacking shipping off Taiwan in October 1944. Other minor changes introduced during production included an additional defensive gun in the tail.

Small numbers of aircraft were completed as the Ki-109 heavy fighter, 22 examples of which received a 75mm cannon in a nose mounting. Meanwhile, conversions of aircraft to undertake kamikaze missions were known as the Mi-67-I Kai, these being operated by a reduced crew of three.

The Allied bombing offensive against Japan curtailed production of the *Hiryu*, which eventually totalled 698 aircraft, of which 606 were built by Mitsubishi, 91 by Kawasaki and one by the Army Air Arsenal at Tachikawa. Although arriving too late in the conflict to make a significant impression, the Ki-67 was heavily utilized in combat during the closing stages of the war, operations in which it was active including attacks on Allied forces on Iwo Jima, the Marianas and Okinawa.

Ki-67-I

Weight Maximum take-off: 13,765kg (30,347lb)

Dimensions Length: 18.70m (61ft 4.25in), Wingspan: 22.50m (73ft 9.75in), Height: 7.70m (25ft 3.25in)

Powerplant Two 1417kW (1900hp) Mitsubishi Ha-104 radial piston engines

Speed 537km/h (334mph) at 6090m (19,980ft)

Range 3800km (2361 miles)

Ceiling 9470m (31,070ft)

Armament 4–5 x 12.7mm (0.5in) machine guns, 1 x 20mm cannon plus a maximum bombload of 800kg (1764lb) or a torpedo up to 1070kg (2359lb)

Ki-67-I

'Peggy' bombers of the 3rd Chutai, 61st Sentai, operated from both mainland China and Taiwan in the final months of the war.

LAND-BASED FIGHTERS

The fighters of the Imperial Japanese Army had proven successful in their encounters with the Chinese in the 1930s, and Japan entered the war in the Pacific with these same aircraft, sharing the same successful attributes of exceptional agility, lightweight construction and relatively light armament.

This chapter includes the following aircraft:

- Nakajima Ki-27 'Nate'
- Nakajima Ki-43 *Hayabusa* 'Oscar'
- Nakajima Ki-44 *Shoki* 'Tojo'
- Kawasaki Ki-45 *Toryu* 'Nick'
- Nakajima J1N *Gekko* 'Irving'
- Kawasaki Ki-61 *Hien* 'Tony'
- Mitsubishi J2M *Raiden* 'Jack'
- Kawanishi N1K-J *Shiden* 'George'
- Nakajima Ki-84 *Hayate* 'Frank'
- Kawasaki Ki-100

Inspired by the interwar Ki-27 design, the nimble Ki-43 would become numerically the most important Imperial Japanese Army Air Service fighter of the Pacific War, but found itself outclassed by Allied designs by 1943.

31

Nakajima Ki-27 'Nate'

Although it sacrificed much in the way of structural robustness and firepower in favour of performance and manoeuvrability, the Ki-27 was a very forward-looking design for its day, and initially, at least, it was a great success in aerial combat.

Beginning life as a private-venture design, the Nakajima PE was a single-seat monoplane fighter that was notably advanced for its time, featuring such innovations as an all-metal stressed-skin construction, constant-speed propeller and flaps.

In mid-1935 the Imperial Japanese Army requested that Nakajima further develop its PE to meet a requirement for a new fighter that would undergo competitive evaluation against designs from Kawasaki and Mitsubishi. The Nakajima aircraft emerged as the Ki-27, the prototype of which shared much commonality with the original PE. The Ki-27 introduced a number of refinements that had been identified after flight-testing the PE. A first flight was achieved in October 1936 and it proved to be the fastest of the three competing designs.

Two prototypes and 10 pre-production examples of the Ki-27 were completed for service evaluation. The pre-series aircraft introduced a wing of increased span and the cockpit received an enclosed canopy. The engine was a 582kW (780hp) Nakajima Kotobuki Ha-1 radial, representing a licence-built Bristol Jupiter. It was in this form that the aircraft was ordered into production in late 1937 as the Army Type 97 Fighter Model A, or Ki-27a.

First blood

When thrown into battle in northern China in March 1938, the Ki-27 initially excelled. Although it lacked self-sealing fuel tanks, armour protection and its firepower was limited to two machine guns, it was capable of out-performing

any fighter in theatre at the time of its appearance in terms of speed, climb and agility. The fighter held air superiority over the Chinese air arms until the introduction of the Soviet-built Polikarpov I-16, which demonstrated speed in excess of its Japanese rival.

Following the outbreak of the war in the Pacific, the Ki-27 saw further combat during the Japanese invasion of Burma, Malaya, the Dutch East Indies and the Philippines. By 1943

Ki-27a

Weight Maximum take-off: 1790kg (3946lb)

Dimensions Length: 7.53m (24ft 8.5in), Wingspan: 11.31m (37ft 1.5in), Height: 7.53m (24ft 8.5in)

Powerplant One 529kW (710hp) Nakajima Ha-1B radial piston engine

Speed 470km/h (292mph) at 3500m (11,485ft)

Range 625km (389 miles)

Ceiling 12,250m (40,190ft)

Armament 2 x 7.7mm (0.303in) machine guns

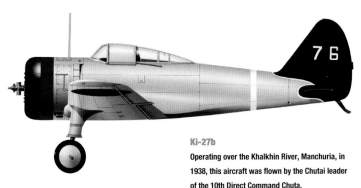

Ki-27b

Operating over the Khalkhin River, Manchuria, in 1938, this aircraft was flown by the Chutai leader of the 10th Direct Command Chuta.

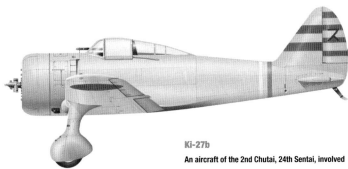

Ki-27b

An aircraft of the 2nd Chutai, 24th Sentai, involved in aerial battles against the Soviet Union during the Nomonhan Incident. In August 1939 it was the personal aircraft of 12-kill ace Goro Nishihara.

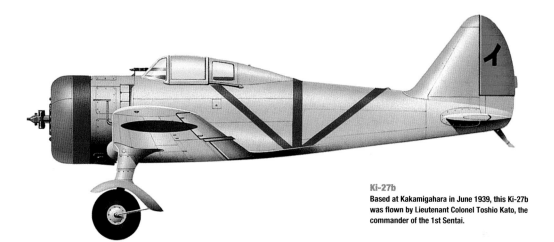

Ki-27b
Based at Kakamigahara in June 1939, this Ki-27b was flown by Lieutenant Colonel Toshio Kato, the commander of the 1st Sentai.

the Ki-27 was becoming increasingly outclassed as a front-line fighter, and survivors were withdrawn to the main islands for homeland defence or used as advanced trainers. Finally, a number were used for kamikaze missions at the end of the conflict.

The only other major production variant was the Ki-27b that introduced slight improvements, including a further refined enclosed cockpit canopy. The experimental Ki-27 Kai that featured a lightened airframe remained in prototype form only, two examples being completed for test work.

Final tally

Production of the Ki-27 continued until 1942, by which time a total of 3399 examples had been manufactured. Of this total, 2020 were completed by Nakajima and 1379 by Mansyu, with a factory located in the puppet state of Manchukuo. Mansyu had assumed responsibility for the Ki-27's production in 1940.

While the initial Allied reporting name 'Abdul' was applied when the Ki-27 was encountered in the China-Burma-India theatre, the type was later reassigned the reporting name 'Nate'.

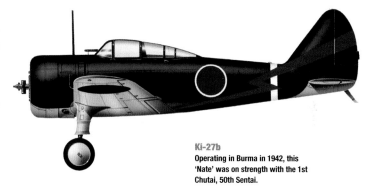

Ki-27b
Operating in Burma in 1942, this 'Nate' was on strength with the 1st Chutai, 50th Sentai.

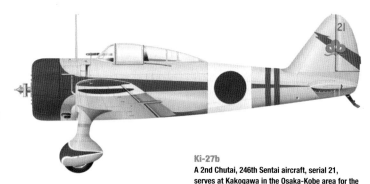

Ki-27b
A 2nd Chutai, 246th Sentai aircraft, serial 21, serves at Kakogawa in the Osaka-Kobe area for the homeland defence of Japan in late 1942.

Nakajima Ki-43 *Hayabusa* 'Oscar'

More examples of the Ki-43 were built than any other Japanese Army fighter, and on its initial appearance in the Pacific War this modern fighter, with its retractable undercarriage, proved a shock to Allied pilots issued with generally inferior equipment.

The Nakajima Ki-43 *Hayabusa* (Peregrine Falcon) was the conceptual successor to the same company's Ki-27, and inherited that aircraft chief attributes of light weight, high performance and exceptional agility.

The design of the Ki-43 was initiated in December 1937 and the first of three prototype designs took to the air in January 1939. Unusually, the aircraft research and development

were the result of a contract placed directly with Nakajima by the Imperial Japanese Army, and without a competitive fly-off with rival designs.

The Ki-43 was a cantilever low-wing monoplane with retractable tailwheel landing gear. The pilot was provided with an enclosed cockpit, and the powerplant was a 727kW (975hp) Nakajima Sakae Ha-25 supercharged engine.

In the pre-series form, the Ki-43 was judged suitable for operational service and duly entered production as the Army Type 1 Fighter Model 1A *Hayabusa*, or Ki-43-Ia. The aircraft's

Ki-43-Ic

This aircraft was flown by the 64th Sentai during initial Japanese attempts to cut off China from the Allied forces in India and Burma.

Ki-43-Ia

Weight Maximum take-off: 2583kg (5695lb)

Dimensions Length: 8.83m (28ft 11.75in), Wingspan: 11.44m (37ft 6.25in), Height: 3.27m (10ft 8.75in)

Powerplant One 727kW (975hp) Nakajima Sakae Ha-25 radial piston engine

Speed 495km/h (308mph) at 4000m (13,125ft)

Range 1200km (745 miles)

Ceiling 11,750m (38,500ft)

Armament 2 x 12.7mm (0.5in) machine guns

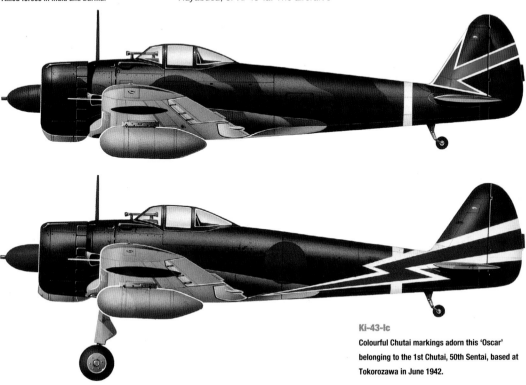

Ki-43-Ic

Colourful Chutai markings adorn this 'Oscar' belonging to the 1st Chutai, 50th Sentai, based at Tokorozawa in June 1942.

Ki-43-II-Otsu

This aircraft was flown by the 3rd Chutai, 25th Sentai, Imperial Japanese Army Air Service, from its base in Hankow, China, in January 1944.

basic armament comprised two forward-firing 7.7mm (0.303in) machine guns in the upper cowling, and it could also carry two 15kg (33lb) bombs. Initially fitted with a two-blade wooden propeller, this was soon replaced by a two-blade metal unit.

At the outbreak of the Pacific War, the Ki-43 represented one of the most capable fighters in theatre. However, once improved Allied fighters began to appear, the basic design of the *Hayabusa* required some refinements to keep pace.

Armament upgrades

The Ki-43-Ib represented an early effort to increase the limited firepower of the initial aircraft, replacing one of the 7.7mm machine guns with a

harder-hitting 12.7mm (0.5in) weapon. Otherwise known as the Army Type 1 Fighter Model 1B, the aircraft was in all other respects similar to its predecessor.

A further boost in firepower arrived with the Ki-43-Ic that introduced an armament of two 12.7mm machine guns. Once again, this was the aircraft's only change compared to the Ki-41-Ia.

Ki-43-II

The first effort to more radically overhaul the *Hayabusa* was the Ki-43-II, which was launched with five prototypes intended to test this version's more powerful Nakajima Ha-115 engine driving a constant-speed three-blade propeller, together with other new additions including self-sealing tanks and armour. The latter two features were the product of early combat experience against the Allies who, although they considered

the *Hayabusa* a tricky opponent, found the aircraft's lack of pilot and fuel protection to be weak points in the basic design. The Ki-43-II was first flown in February 1942 and yielded five prototypes and three identical pre-series aircraft.

In November 1942 the Ki-43-II entered production as the Ki-43-IIa, or Army Type 1 Fighter Model 2A, which retained the twin 12.7mm machine gun armament of the Ki-43-Ic. However, the new model introduced an improved ground-attack capability, with underwing carriage for two 250kg (551lb) bombs. Other changes included a revised supercharger intake in the upper lip of the cowling (rather than in the 'chin' position), reduced wingspan and wing area, revised

Ki-43-IIa

One of a small number of Ki-43s delivered to the Manchukuo Army Air Corps, operated by the puppet state of Manchuoko.

windscreen and canopy and a new reflector gunsight.

The Ki-43-IIb was broadly similar to the Ki-43-IIa but with minor equipment changes. In the event, the Ki-43-IIb quickly replaced the IIa as the standard production version, and in its initial form the IIb differed only in relation to changes made to the carburettor intake. However, the late-production Ki-43-IIb introduced other distinguishing features, including wing

hardpoints moved further outboard, and eventually an oil cooler relocated from the carburettor intake to below the centre fuselage.

Once the various improvements of the Ki-43-IIa and Ki-43-IIb had been unified and introduced on the production line, the result was known

as the Ki-43-II Kai. Compared to earlier aircraft, the Ki-43-II Kai also introduced individual exhaust stacks for an increase in thrust.

Ki-43-III

The next major change for the *Hayabusa* took the form of another new powerplant, the Ha-115-II. The new engine was tested in a total of 10 prototypes of the Ki-43-IIIa version, the first of which was completed in May 1944. While the new engine produced more power at altitude, the aircraft otherwise remained essentially unchanged from the Ki-43-II Kai. Although quantity production was not undertaken by Nakajima, the Ki-43-IIIa was built in series by Tachikawa as the Army Type 1 Fighter Model 3A.

Ki-43-IIb

Two views of a colourful aircraft flown by the leader of the Headquarters Chutai of the 77th Sentai during operations in Burma in the winter of 1943/44.

Ki-43-IIb

Weight Maximum take-off: 2590kg (5710lb)
Dimensions Length: 8.92m (29ft 3.25in), Wingspan: 10.84m (35ft 6.75in), Height: 3.27m (10ft 8.75in)
Powerplant One 858kW (1150hp) Nakajima Ha-115 radial piston engine
Speed 530km/h (329mph) at 4000m (13,125ft)
Range 3200km (1988 miles)
Ceiling 11,200m (36,745ft)
Armament 2 x 12.7mm (0.5in) machine guns plus up to 2 x 250kg (551lb) bombs underwing

---

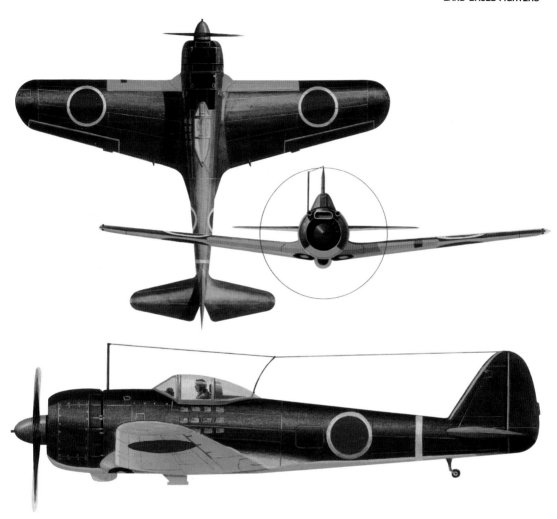

The Ki-43-IIIb promised to be the ultimate *Hayabusa*, with a 932kW (1250hp) Mitsubishi Ha-112 engine allied with forward-firing armament of two 20mm cannon, while the underwing bomb racks of the Ki-43-IIa were retained. Only two prototypes were completed, and the version did not enter quantity production.

Production run

The *Hayabusa* manufacturing effort came to an end with a total of 5919 aircraft built. As well as 3239 planes built by the original manufacturer, a further 2631 were produced by Tachikawa Aircraft Company Limited and another 49 by the 1st Army Air Arsenal. All versions received the Allied reporting name 'Oscar'.

The aircraft was the most numerous in the Army inventory, and served in all theatres of the conflict throughout the Pacific. First seeing service over Burma and the Malaya Peninsula in the opening weeks of the Pacific

Ki-43–II Kai

Three views of a Ki-43-II Kai, representing the penultimate production version, and the last of which to be manufactured by the parent company.

War, the *Hayabusa* ended the conflict flying missions in the defence of the homeland, either as a bomber interceptor or on the feared kamikaze suicide raids. The Ki-43's service continued after World War II, when it was flown by the French in Indo-China and by Indonesia.

Nakajima Ki-44 *Shoki* 'Tojo'

As the fastest-climbing Japanese fighter of World War II to see quantity production, the Ki-44 interceptor held the line in the defence of the homeland when the US Army Air Force began its bombing offensive with the B-29 Superfortress.

Known as the *Shoki* (Demon), the Nakajima Ki-44 interceptor had the appearance of a beefed-up Ki-43, and was strongly influenced by the company's previous fighter design. Compared to the Ki-43, however, the design of the Ki-44 stressed speed and rate of climb rather than agility, which made it ideal for the bomber-interceptor mission in which it would see most of its service. Design and development of the Ki-44 was more or less contemporaneous with that of the Ki-43, but the project differed in its requirements, the

specification calling for the ability to climb to 4000m (13,125ft) in less than five minutes, and a top speed of 600km/h (373mph).

In its initial form, the Ki-44 was powered by a 932kW (1250hp) Nakajima Ha-41 radial engine, this being chosen as the most powerful powerplant then available. In terms of configuration, the Ki-44 was otherwise broadly similar to the Ki-43. The prototype and pre-production aircraft were armed with two 7.7mm (0.303in) and two 12.7mm (0.5in) machine guns.

First flown in prototype form in

Ki-44-IIb

Weight Maximum take-off: 2995kg (6603lb)

Dimensions Length: 8.80m (28ft 10.5in), Wingspan: 9.45m (31ft), Height: 3.25m (10ft 8in)

Powerplant One 1133kW (1520hp) Nakajima Ha-109 radial piston engine

Speed 605km/h (376mph) at 5200m (17,060ft)

Range 1700km (1056 miles)

Ceiling 11,200m (36,745ft)

Armament 4 x 12.7mm (0.5in) machine guns

Ki-44 (pre-series)

A pre-production Ki-44 that was utilized for combat trials by the 47th Dokuritsu Chutai in Malaya in early 1942.

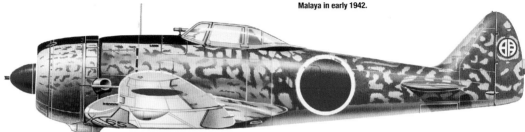

Ki-44-I

This aircraft was assigned to an Air Training Division at Akeno airfield, Mie prefecture, in 1944.

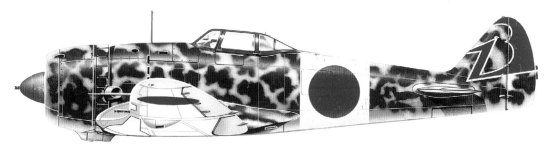

August 1940, the Ki-44 successfully underwent pre-service trials (seven pre-production aircraft were completed, the last in September 1941) and the aircraft was approved for production as the Army Type 2 Single-seat Fighter Model 1A *Shoki*, or Ki-44-Ia. The fighter was officially adopted for service in September 1942 after trials with an experimental unit based in China.

The armament of the Army Type 2 Single-seat Fighter Model 1B, or Ki-44-Ib, was revised with all four weapons now of 12.7mm calibre. Another change involved moving the oil cooler from inside the engine cowling to a position below the cowling gills.

The last of the Model 1 series was the Ki-44-Ic, which featured modifications to the mainwheel fairings. Only a small number of these aircraft were completed, and total manufacture of the entire Model 1 series only extended to 40 production airframes.

Changing fortunes

Once issued to service units, the Ki-44 was initially unpopular. Possessing comparatively high wing loading, the *Shoki* was found to suffer from high landing speeds and limited manoeuvrability. Ultimately, however, the aircraft was praised for its performance, especially when pitted against the Allied bombing offensive.

The first significant overhaul of the *Shoki* was the Ki-44-II, the five prototypes and three pre-production

Ki-44-IIb

An example of the 'Tojo' used for homeland defence in late 1944. The operating unit was the 23rd Sentai, and the aircraft served in the Eastern Defence Sector.

examples of which, completed beginning in August 1942, were distinguished by their new powerplant, a more powerful Ha-109 engine. This was intended to boost performance since although the original Ki-44 was the fastest Army fighter at the time, it was still slower than the Mitsubishi Ki-46 reconnaissance aircraft.

The Ki-44-II entered production and service as the Ki-44-IIa, which retained the armament of the Ki-44-Ia. However, only a small number of these were

PILOT IMPRESSIONS

When first fielded, the Ki-44 was somewhat unpopular among Army pilots, used as they were to more lightweight and agile aircraft. Compared to its predecessors it lacked for manoeuvrability and its high landing speed could be hazardous. However, once pilots moved direct from training on to the Shoki, the fighter's fortunes improved and these new pilots began to better exploit its rapid rate of climb and diving speed. On the other hand, snap rolls, stalls, spins and high-speed inverted flight were restricted, and the fighter's pilot protection and self-sealing tanks were found wanting.

Although it was the only Japanese Army interceptor in service when the USAAF launched its B-29 raids on the Japanese home islands, just three Sentais were still equipped with the fast-climbing Ki-44 by the end of the war.

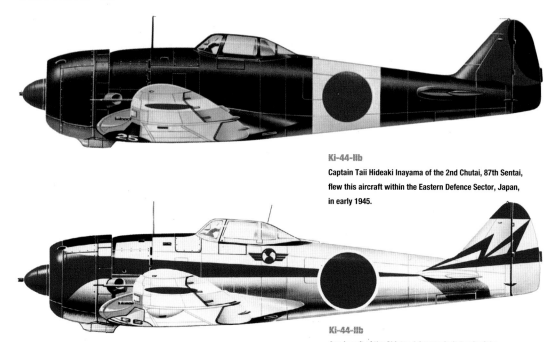

Ki-44-IIb

Captain Taii Hideaki Inayama of the 2nd Chutai, 87th Sentai, flew this aircraft within the Eastern Defence Sector, Japan, in early 1945.

Ki-44-IIb

An aircraft of the Shinten (air superiority) unit of the 47th Sentai, based at Narimasu, Tokyo, in summer 1944.

completed before the production line standardized on the next sub-variant.

For the major production version of the Ki-44-II, the Army Type 2 Single-seat Fighter Model 2B, or Ki-44-IIb, the armament was revised such that it was the same as that of the Ki-44-Ib; the remainder of the airframe was identical to that of the Ki-44-Ic.

'Tojo' in action

The Ki-44-IIb began to spearhead defensive interceptor operations over the Japanese homeland after the attacks by B-25 bombers launched from the carrier USS *Hornet* in April 1942. The aircraft were also stationed in China, Malaya and Burma, while in Sumatra they were assigned to the protection of vital oilfields.

The armament of the *Shoki* was further altered with the Ki-44-IIc, which offered firepower in the form of four

20mm cannon. In this guise, the Shoko was a formidable bomber-destroyer, able to tackle the B-29 raids directed against Japan. As an alternative the Ki-44-IIc could be armed with two 40mm cannon and two 12.7mm machine guns. However, since the effective range of the heavy 40mm cannon was so short, some Ki-44-IIc aircraft were instead armed with two 37mm weapons, which offered a greater range.

A new engine was introduced in the 'third-generation' *Shoki*, the Ki-43-III, which entered production as the Ki-44-IIIa, powered by a 1491kW (2000hp) Nakajima Ha-145 radial engine with thrust-augmentation stacks. Standard armament was four 20mm cannon.

Other changes included increased wing area and enlarged tail surfaces to help offset increased weight from the new engine. First flown in June 1943,

the aircraft was built in small numbers only, with the Army favouring the Nakajima Ki-84-I.

The final production version was the Ki-44-IIIb, which was similar to the Ki-44-IIIa but with a revised 'bomber-destroyer' armament of two 20mm cannon and two 37mm cannon.

The total production of the Ki-44 family amounted to 1225 aircraft when manufacture ceased in late 1944, when it was superseded in production by the Ki-84. All aircraft were built by Nakajima and were given the Allied reporting name 'Tojo'.

At the end of the war, at least one *Shoki* unit became a specialist kamikaze air defence squadron. This, the Shinten Seikutai of the 47th Sentai, used its aircraft for ramming attacks against American bombers, with some success during the defence of Tokyo in November 1944.

Kawasaki Ki-45 *Toryu* 'Nick'

Ultimately serving in the defence of the homeland as a night-fighter, the Ki-45 was originally drafted as a long-range heavy fighter. Inspired by Western designs of the mid-1930s, the Ki-45's path to operational service with the IJA would prove tortuous.

While the Nakajima Ki-44 was fielded as the Army Type 2 Single-seat Fighter, the Army Type 2 Two-seat Fighter was the Ki-45 from the designers at Kawasaki. Named *Toryu* (Dragon-Killer), the origins of the Ki-45 date back to early 1937, when the Imperial Japanese Army issued a specification calling for design and development of a twin-engine fighter that would have the endurance to conduct operations over the Pacific.

Development work on the new fighter was initiated under the designation Ki-38, but after significant changes were incorporated this was revised to become Ki-45. This was a cantilever mid-wing monoplane with retractable landing gear. The fuselage provided accommodation for two crew in tandem enclosed cockpits.

Initial prototype

A first prototype Ki-45 took to the air for the first time in January 1939. In its initial form, the prototype was powered by a pair of Nakajima Ha-20B radial engines, but these 611kW (820hp) units failed to meet their rated power. Initial armament of the first three prototypes comprised three 7.7mm (0.303in) machine guns and one 20mm cannon.

Once re-engined with 746kW (1000hp) Nakajima Ha-25 radials, a new prototype received the designation Ki-45-I, although armament remained unchanged. Introduction of a new

Ki-45 Kai-c

Weight Maximum take-off: 5500kg (12,125lb)
Dimensions Length: 11.00m (36ft 1in), Wingspan: 15.05m (49ft 4.5in), Height: 3.70m (12ft 1.5in)
Powerplant Two 805kW (1080hp) Mitsubishi Ha-102 radial piston engines
Speed 545km/h (339mph) at 7000m (22,965ft)
Range 2000km (1243 miles)
Ceiling 10,000m (32,810ft)
Armament 1 x 7.92mm (0.31in) aft-firing machine gun, 2 x 20mm forward-firing cannon and 1 x 37mm forward-firing cannon

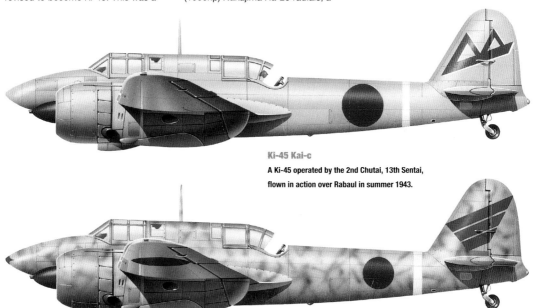

Ki-45 Kai-c
A Ki-45 operated by the 2nd Chutai, 13th Sentai, flown in action over Rabaul in summer 1943.

Ki-45 Kai-c
An aircraft of the Hombu Sentai, 21st Sentai, that was based at Palembang, Sumatra, in May 1945.

powerplant – which faced substantial development problems of its own – resulted in a delay to the programme, and it was not until July 1940 that the improved Ki-45, formally known as Experimental Improved Type 1 Ki-45, took to the air.

Finally, the generally improved Ki-45 Kai design was ordered into production as the Army Type 2 Two-seat Fighter Model A *Toryu*, otherwise known as the Ki-45 Kai-a, in September 1941. Introduced to service in August 1942, the aircraft first saw combat in October 1942 after which it was given the Allied reporting name 'Nick'.

The Ki-45 found early success against the US Army Air Force's B-24 bombers, and when these were adapted for night operations the 'Nick' was similarly modified to counter them; some received upward-firing 7.7mm

(0.303in) machine guns to attack the bombers from below. The success of the night-fighter adaptation led to the design of a dedicated version for this mission.

The night-fighter 'Nick' was the Ki-45 Kai-c, armed with a 37mm cannon in the ventral tunnel and two obliquely mounted upward-firing 20mm cannon. The nose was to receive a radar, but development had not been completed when the war ended.

The improved Ka-45-II (later designated Ki-96) was a projected single-seat derivative.

Production of the Ki-45 amounted to 1698 aircraft of all versions. Theatres in which the Ki-45 saw notable action included Burma, Manchuria and Sumatra. Towards the end of the war, the Ki-45 was adapted for kamikaze operations.

GROUND-ATTACK VERSIONS

Soon after the Ki-45 Kai-a had been fielded as a heavy fighter, efforts were made to produce a sub-variant dedicated to ground-attack roles. This was the Ki-45 Kai-b, or Army Type 2 Two-seat Fighter Model B, which had revised forward-firing armament of one 20mm cannon in the nose and one hand-loaded 37mm cannon in the ventral tunnel. Another aircraft received an experimental installation with a 75mm cannon for anti-tank work, while the Ki-45 Kai-d was a specialist anti-shipping aircraft with two 20mm nose cannon, one 37mm cannon in the central tunnel and one defensive machine gun in the rear cockpit.

Ki-45 Kai-c

An aircraft of the 1st Chutai, 5th Sentai, based at
Kashiwa, Chiba Prefecture, in spring 1943.

Ki-45 Kai-c

This aircraft flew with the 2nd Chutai,
27th Sentai, based in the Philippines
in November 1944.

Nakajima J1N *Gekko* 'Irving'

Originally designed as a heavy escort fighter, the J1N went through several iterations, including reconnaissance aircraft, before it emerged as a night-fighter for the Imperial Japanese Navy, serving in this role with some distinction until the end of the war.

First flown in prototype form in May 1941, the Nakajima J1N was designed to meet an Imperial Japanese Navy requirement for a long-range fighter. The aircraft was originally intended for use in an offensive capacity, escorting bombers on missions deep into China.

The Nakajima J1N was a cantilever low-wing monoplane with retractable tailwheel landing gear, and was powered by a pair of Nakajima Sakae 21/22 counter-rotating engines. The fuselage had accommodation for a crew of three, and armament comprised three 7.7mm (0.303in) machine guns and one 20mm cannon.

Once under test, it was revealed that the aircraft was not best suited to the escort fighter role, offering little that was superior to the Mitsubishi A6M other than range. Instead, the design was reworked for the long-range reconnaissance role under the designation J1N1-C.

The J1N1-C differed in having two Sakae 21 engines and the armament was revised to comprise a single rear-firing 7.7mm weapon. At the same time,

internal fuel consumption was reduced, but provision was added for external drop tanks.

After seven prototypes of the J1N1-C completed pre-service trials, the aircraft was ordered into production as the Navy Type 2 Reconnaissance Aircraft, and later received the revised shortened designation J1N1-R. Not long after, a number of the aircraft were fitted with revised armament, replacing the rear-firing machine gun with a 20mm cannon. These aircraft were designated as the J1N1-F.

Night-fighter role

In early 1943 it was suggested that the aircraft could provide a platform for the development of a night-fighter version. For this role, the crew was reduced from three to two and armament was increased, with four 20mm cannon mounted obliquely in pairs in dorsal and ventral positions, two firing upwards and two firing downwards.

The initial night-fighter conversion proved successful in its encounters with B-24 bombers, and further

J1N1-S

Weight Maximum take-off: 8185kg (18,045lb)
Dimensions Length: 12.77m (41ft 10.75in), Wingspan: 16.98m (55ft 8.25in), Height: 3.99m (13ft 1.5in)
Powerplant Two 843kW (1130hp) Nakajima Sakae 21 radial piston engines
Speed 507km/h (315mph) at 5800m (19,030ft)
Range 3780km (2348 miles)
Ceiling 9320m (30,580ft)
Armament 4 x 20mm cannon in obliquely mounted upwards- and downwards-firing pairs

conversions were authorized as the J1N1-C Kai.

A production version of the night-fighter, the J1N1-S *Gekko* (Moonlight) could be equipped with a small searchlight in the nose and later-production aircraft were fitted with a basic air-interception radar.

The J1N1-Sa version was another night-fighter, this time with the ineffective downward-firing cannon deleted. In some cases, these aircraft received an additional forward-firing cannon in the nose. Production of all models amounted to 479 aircraft.

J1N1-C Kai

This J1N1-C Kai night-fighter served with the 251st Kokutai, based at Lakunari, Rabaul, in November 1943.

Kawasaki Ki-61 *Hien* 'Tony'

Unique among Japanese fighters of World War II on account of its inline piston powerplant, the Ki-61 was developed under the influence of German designers, but persistent powerplant issues continued to undermine the *Hien* (Swallow).

The design of the Kawasaki Ki-61 was based around the same company's Ha-40 inline piston engine, a licence-built version of the German Daimler-Benz DB 601A. A first Japanese-built version of the engine was completed in July 1941. This engine was flown in the prototype Ki-60, but it proved to be altogether unsuccessful.

The powerplant was retained for a new design, the Ki-61, which first flew in prototype form in December 1941. Ultimately, a total of 12 prototypes were used for test work.

Sharing much in common with the Messerschmitt Bf 109, the Allies initially reported that the Ki-61 was a licence-built version of the German fighter, or perhaps a variant of an unspecified Italian fighter. In its initial form, the Ki-61 was armed with two wing-mounted 7.7mm (0.303in) or 12.7mm (0.5in)

machine guns and two fuselage-mounted 12.7mm machine guns, marking a significant boost in firepower over the Ki-43-I that was then entering service. Critically, the Ki-61 was among the first Japanese fighters to incorporate self-sealing fuel tanks and armour protection for the pilot from the

Ki-61-lc

Weight Maximum take-off: 3470kg (7650lb)
Dimensions Length: 8.95m (29ft 4.25in),
Wingspan: 12.00m (39ft 4.5in), Height: 3.70m
(12ft 1.75in)
Powerplant One 876kW (1175hp) Kawasaki Ha-40
inline piston engine
Speed 560km/h (348mph)
Range 1900km (1181 miles)
Ceiling 10,000m (32,810ft)
Armament 2 x 12.7mm (0.5in) machine guns
and 2 x 20mm cannon

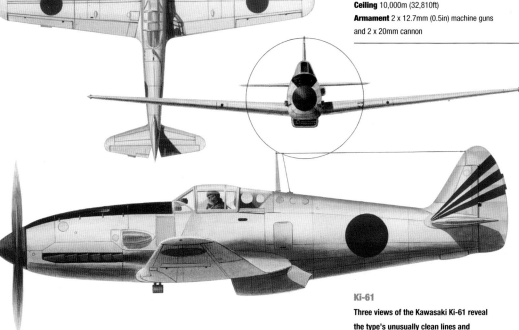

Ki-61

Three views of the Kawasaki Ki-61 reveal the type's unusually clean lines and aerodynamic profile.

outset. The use of a high-aspect ratio wing of generous area was intended to ensure the fighter's manoeuvrability and long range.

Pre-service trials of the Ki-61 were successful, and the aircraft was ordered into production for the Imperial Japanese Army as the Army Type 3 Fighter Model 1 *Hien*, or Ki-61-I. The aircraft received the Allied reporting name 'Tony'.

Entering combat in New Guinea in April 1943, the Ki-61 was a good match for the Allied fighters it encountered at the time. The Ki-61 quickly showed itself to be superior to the Ki-43, with advantages in terms of armament, protection and diving speed. The major disadvantage was the performance of the inline engine when taxiing on the ground, especially in 'hot and high' conditions. Ultimately, production was increased such that the *Hien* could be found in all major theatres of combat in the Pacific.

Armament variations

In its first production guise, two distinct sub-variants of the Ki-61-I were manufactured. The first of these was the Ki-61-Ia (Army Type 3 Fighter Model 1A), with two fuselage-mounted 12.7mm (0.303in) and two wing-mounted 7.7mm (0.5in) machine guns. The Ki-61-Ib (Model 1B), meanwhile, featured 12.7mm machine guns in the wing and fuselage.

In some of the Ki-61-Ia and Ki-61-Ib aircraft, the wing machine guns were replaced with German-supplied Mauser 20mm cannon, these being fitted on the production line in the absence of similar Japanese-made weapons.

In the Ki-61-Ic, armament changes were introduced in an effort to ease maintenance; the two wing-mounted weapons remained 12.7mm machine guns, while the fuselage-mounted weapons were replaced with Japanese-made 20mm cannon. At the same time, the basic structure of the *Hien*

Ki-61-Ib

An aircraft of the 3rd Chutai, 59th Sentai, based at Ashiya, in August 1945. The replacement of the rear fuselage and rudder has resulted in a hybrid tail insignia (22nd Sentai and Akeno Flying Training School).

Ki-61-Ib

An aircraft of the 1st Chutai, 244th Sentai, led by Major Kobayashi and stationed at Chofu and Narumatsu in 1945. Captain Takada was the 1st Chutai leader.

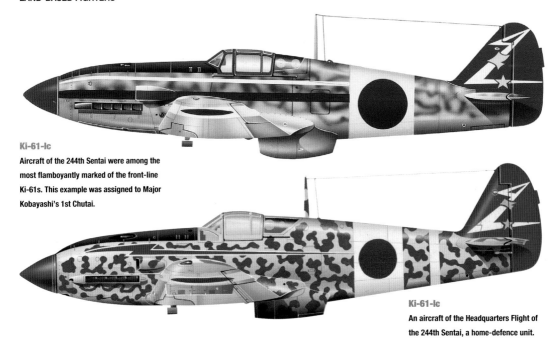

Ki-61-Ic
Aircraft of the 244th Sentai were among the most flamboyantly marked of the front-line Ki-61s. This example was assigned to Major Kobayashi's 1st Chutai.

Ki-61-Ic
An aircraft of the Headquarters Flight of the 244th Sentai, a home-defence unit.

was simplified and strengthened to improve serviceability in battlefield conditions. The stronger wings allowed an improvement in diving speed, and permitted carriage of external stores. Another change was the introduction of a fixed rather than retractable tailwheel.

The Ki-61-Ic entered production in January 1944 and swiftly superseded the previous two versions on the production line. Also known as the Ki-61-I Kai-c, the new aircraft was being built at a rate of over 250 per month by July 1944.

Finally, the Ki-61-Id (Ki-61-I Kai-d), built in small numbers only, introduced more powerful weapons, with the wing machine guns giving way to two 30mm cannon of Japanese manufacture; in addition a pair of 12.7mm machine guns were fitted in the wings.

Ki-61-II series
In an effort to overhaul the *Hien*, Kawasaki launched development of

an improved Ki-61-II, the first prototype of which was completed in December 1943. A total of eight prototype Ki-61-II aircraft were built, their main role being to test the installation of the new and more powerful Kawasaki Ha-140 engine and a new wing of increased area. Other changes included a modified cockpit canopy offering improved visibility for the pilot. However, not only did the Ha-140 suffer from teething troubles but the revised wing was also found to be prone to failure. Before the 'second series' was launched into production, a total of 30 pre-production aircraft were completed under the designation Ki-61-II Kai, these reverting to the original Ki-61-I wing and with redesigned tail surfaces.

Once in production, which commenced in September 1944, the new aircraft was fielded with two distinct armament configurations. Designated Ki-61-IIa (Army Type 3 Fighter Model 2A), the first of these

featured armament of two fuselage-mounted 20mm cannon and two wing-mounted 12.7mm machine guns. The Ki-61-IIb (Model 2B) was otherwise similar to the Ki-61-IIa, but featured an armament consisting of four 20mm cannon, two each mounted in the fuselage and wings.

Engine troubles
However, due to continued problems with the powerplant, the Ki-61-II Kai never succeeded in replacing the Ki-61-I, and only a relatively small number of the 'second generation' fighter saw active service. In its favour, however, was its high-altitude performance, which meant the Ki-61-II was one of the most effective counters to the US Army Air Force's B-29 raids; in tests, the Ki-61-II demonstrated a climb to 5000m (16,405ft) in six minutes.

In January 1945, production of the Ki-61-II was brought to a standstill by USAAF raids against Akashi in the

Hyogo Prefecture where production of the Ha-140 engine was centred.

A single example of a planned 'third generation' *Hien* was manufactured, as the Ki-61-III. A single aerodynamic prototype was completed before focus switched to the Kawasaki Ki-100 (see below), which replaced the inline engine with a radial unit.

By the time production came to an end, a total of 3078 examples of the Ki-61 had been built. Of these, the vast majority were Ki-61-I and Ki-61-I Kai versions, while a total of 374 aircraft were built as Ki-61-II aircraft, of which 275 were ultimately completed as Ki-100-Ia fighters (described separately).

Service

As well as fighting extensively round New Guinea and Rabaul, the *Hien* was widely employed during the campaign in the Philippines and over Taiwan and Okinawa. Towards the end of the war, the Ki-61 was increasingly assigned to homeland defence duties, featuring prominently in the aerial battles around Tokyo. Such was the quality of the basic fighter that it continued to hold its own against all Allied fighter opposition until the arrival of the superlative P-51 Mustang, flying from Iwo Jima.

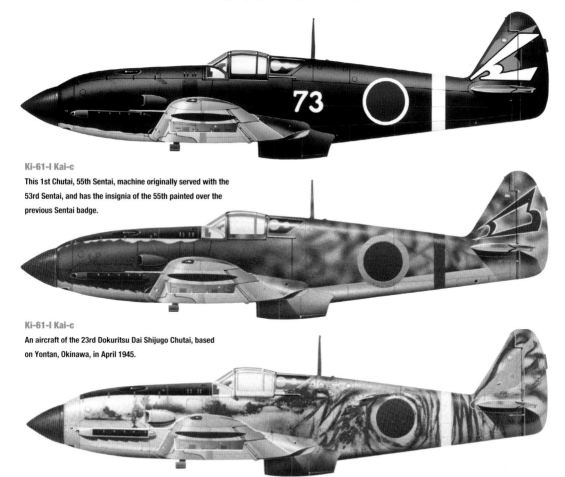

Ki-61-I Kai-c

This 1st Chutai, 55th Sentai, machine originally served with the 53rd Sentai, and has the insignia of the 55th painted over the previous Sentai badge.

Ki-61-I Kai-c

An aircraft of the 23rd Dokuritsu Dai Shijugo Chutai, based on Yontan, Okinawa, in April 1945.

Ki-61-I Kai-c

A hastily applied green 'mottle' camouflage is worn by this 'Tony' of the 3rd Chutai, 19th Sentai, which fought in the Philippines as well as Taiwan and Okinawa.

Mitsubishi J2M *Raiden* 'Jack'

A powerful land-based interceptor for the Imperial Japanese Navy, the *Raiden* (Thunderbolt) originated in a design that stressed speed and rate of climb rather than agility, and saw its most important service in the defence of the Japanese homeland.

In 1938 the Imperial Japanese Navy put out a requirement for a single-seat interceptor, leading to the manufacture of three prototypes of the J2M1 by Mitsubishi. The first example took to the air in March 1942.

A cantilever low-wing monoplane with retractable tailwheel landing gear, the J2M1 was a forward-looking design but one that would be bogged down by developmental delays. Above all, the availability of engines would prove a problem for the aircraft once wartime demands put availability at a premium.

In its initial form, the J2M1 was powered by a 1066kW (1430hp)

Mitsubishi Kasei 13 radial engine, this large-diameter unit featuring an extension shaft between the engine and the reduction gear to ensure that it could be accommodated within the nose nacelle.

Powered by the Kasei 13, the J2M1 was found wanting in initial tests, failing to meet the Navy's requirements for maximum speed and rate of climb. This led to the aircraft being re-engined with a 1357kW (1820hp) Mitsubishi MK4R-A Kasei 23a engine, after which the aircraft was designated as the J2M2.

In J2M2 form, the aircraft was ordered into production in October 1942 as the Navy Interceptor Fighter *Raiden* Model 11. However, the powerplant was still proving to be troublesome, and the J2M2 did not finally enter Imperial Japanese Navy service until December 1943.

The J2M3 version became the major production model, which featured revised armament and led to the J2M3a with further revised

RAIDEN AT WAR
Development problems meant that the Raiden was slow to arrive in service; only 14 aircraft had been delivered by March 1943, six months after production had been approved. Initial deliveries of the J2M2 began to the 381st Kokutai at Toyohashi, Aichi Prefecture. By that time, the J2M3 had emerged as the major production variant, and this was deployed to the Philippines where the aircraft received the Allied reporting name 'Jack'. Thereafter, the bulk of the type's combat service would be recorded over the Japanese home islands, where it excelled as a bomber-destroyer.

armament, the J2M4 (two prototypes only) with turbocharged engine, the J2M5 powered by a 1357kW (1820hp) Mitsubishi MK4U-4 radial, the J2M5a with armament changes and the single J2M6 that was a J2M3 with revised cockpit. Total production amounted to 476 aircraft of all versions.

J2M3
Weight Maximum take-off: 3945kg (8695lb)
Dimensions Length: 9.95m (32ft 7.75in), Wingspan: 10.82m (35ft 5.25in), Height: 3.95m (12ft 11.5in)
Powerplant One 1357kW (1820hp) Mitsubishi MK4R-A Kasei 23a radial piston engine
Speed 595km/h (370mph) at 5900m (19,360ft)
Range 1055km (655 miles)
Ceiling 11,700m (38,385ft)
Armament 4 x 20mm cannon plus two 60kg (132lb) bombs on underwing racks

J2M3

A Raiden flown by the Navy's 302nd Kokuati, based in Japan in 1945.

Kawanishi N1K-J *Shiden* 'George'

A landplane development of a floatplane fighter, the N1K series was built to the tune of 1435 aircraft of all variants, but the early decision to introduce a new powerplant to the basic airframe meant the interceptor was dogged by problems throughout its career.

N1K2-J

A late-production Shiden Kai of the 343rd Kokutai,
Imperial Japanese Navy Air Force, during 1945.

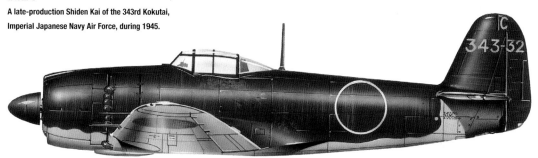

In 1942 Kawanishi began developing a land-based version of its N1K1 *Kyofu* (Mighty Wind) floatplane fighter under the designation N1K1-J.

While the new aircraft retained the airframe of the floatplane, it received a new powerplant in the form of the 1357kW (1820hp) Nakajima NK9H Homare 11 engine. The choice of this new engine would serve to complicate the aircraft's development and service and led to the requirement to fit a large-diameter propeller, which in turn required telescopic main landing gear units.

As first flown, however, in December 1942, the N1K1-J revealed superb performance and manoeuvrability, and a strenuous effort was made to bring the new fighter into Navy service. Finally, at the end of 1943 the aircraft was rewarded with a production order, under the designation Navy Interceptor Fighter *Shiden* (Violet Lightning).

In early 1944 the first examples of the N1K1-J reached frontline service, but by this time work was already well under way on a definitive fighter

version, the N1K2-J, work on which began in mid-1943.

Production derivatives of the original N1K1-J included the N1K1-Ja with armament of four 20mm cannon, and no machine guns; the N1K1-Jb with four 20mm cannon in the wings and provision for two 250kg (551lb) bombs underwing; and the N1K1-Jc with increased capacity for external stores, allowing carriage of up to four 250kg (551lb) weapons.

Further developments

While the N1K1-J was destined to remain an interim aircraft, the N1K2-J represented a major redesign, with the wing moved from the mid-fuselage to a lower-fuselage position, a lengthened fuselage, revised tail surfaces and new, less complex main undercarriage units. Although it was still far from reliable the Nakajima NK9H engine was retained.

In this form, the N1K2-J was first flown in December 1943 and was approved for production as the Navy Interceptor Fighter *Shiden* Kai. Development of the *Shiden* Kai

N1K2-J

Weight Maximum take-off: 4860kg (10,714lb)
Dimensions Length: 9.35m (30ft 8in), Wingspan: 12.00m (39ft 4.5in), Height: 3.96m (13ft)
Powerplant One 1484kW (1820hp) Nakajima NK9H Homare 21 radial piston engine
Speed 595km/h (370mph) at 5600m (18,370ft)
Range 2335km (1451 miles)
Ceiling 10,760m (35,300ft)
Armament 4 x 20mm cannon plus two 250kg (551lb) bombs on underwing racks

continued until the end of the war, resulting in variants including the N1K2-K two-seat trainer.

Derivatives that did not see quantity production included the N1K3-J (two prototypes) with the engine moved forwards to improve stability and with two additional machine guns; the N1K3-A proposed carrier version of the N1K3-J; the N1K4-J (two prototypes) with 1491kW (2000hp) Homare 23 engine; the N1K4-A (one prototype) carrier version of the N1K4-J; and the N1K5-J (one prototype) with 1641kW (2200hp) Mitsubishi MK9A engine.

Nakajima Ki-84 *Hayate* 'Frank'

The finest Japanese fighter to see large-scale service during World War II, the Ki-84 offered a superb balance of agility, speed and firepower and it was afforded highest-priority production status as Japan's military was forced on to the defensive from 1944.

Known as the *Hayate* (Gale), the Nakajima Ki-84 started life in early 1942 when the manufacturer began to design a new interceptor fighter and fighter-bomber to replace the Ki-43 *Hayabusa*. The first of a total of two Ki-84 prototypes was completed in March 1943 and took to the air for the first time one month later. The pair underwent successful testing before Nakajima began work on a batch of 83 service trials aircraft and 42 pre-production machines.

While these aircraft had a top speed below that specified in the original requirements, pilots were quick to highlight the aircraft's excellent levels of performance and protection.

Into production

In late 1943 the Ki-84 was authorized for full-scale production as the Army Type 4 Fighter Model 1A *Hayate*, or Ki-84-Ia. In common with the trials and pre-production aircraft, this initial production model featured an armament of two 12.7mm (0.5in) machine guns in the fuselage and two wing-mounted 20mm cannon. Otherwise, the aircraft was a conventional low-wing monoplane

Ki-84-Ia

Weight Maximum take-off: 3890kg (8576lb)
Dimensions Length: 9.92m (32ft 6.5in), Wingspan: 11.24m (36ft 10.5in), Height: 3.39m (11ft 1.5in)
Powerplant One 1416kW (1900hp) Nakajima Ha-45 radial piston engine
Speed 631km/h (392mph) at 6120m (20,080ft)
Range 2168km (1347 miles)
Ceiling 10,500m (35,350ft)
Armament 2 x 12.7mm (0.5in) machine guns cannon, 2 x 20mm cannon plus two 250kg (551lb) bombs on underwing racks

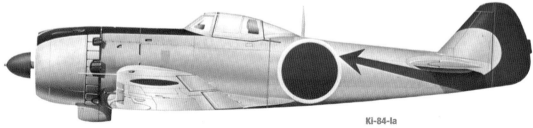

Ki-84-Ia
This 'Frank' served with the 29th Sentai on the island of Taiwan in August 1945. Blue fin markings indicate the HQ Chutai.

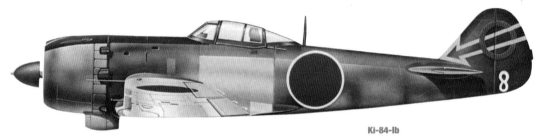

Ki-84-Ib
The 102nd Hiko Sentai operated from Kyushu and was established in late 1944, seeing action in the Okinawa Campaign.

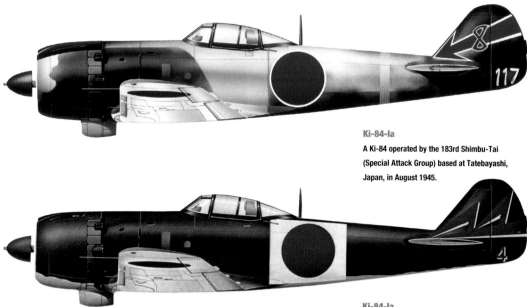

Ki-84-Ia

A Ki-84 operated by the 183rd Shimbu-Tai (Special Attack Group) based at Tatebayashi, Japan, in August 1945.

Ki-84-Ia

In August 1945, this *Hayate* was assigned to the 1st Chutai of the 47th Sentai, based at Narumatsu.

with its tailplane set characteristically ahead of its vertical tail surfaces.

As production continued, the Ki-84-Ib (Army Type 4 Fighter Model 1B) introduced revised armament, with the two fuselage-mounted machine guns giving way to two 20mm cannon for a total of four.

The Ki-84-Ic (Model C) introduced heavier armament in the form of two fuselage-mounted 20mm cannon and two wing-mounted 30mm cannon. Equipped with this firepower it was tailored for the bomber-destroyer mission. Once in service, the Ki-84-II was offered with the same armament options as the Ki-84-Ib and Ki-84-Ic.

In an effort to improve the serviceability of the Ki-84, the original Nakajima Ha-45 (Model 21) radial engine was superseded by the same company's Ha-45 (Model 23), which was less vulnerable to loss of fuel pressure and which incorporated a fuel-injection system. However, the

powerplant suffered a blow when the production facility at Musashi fell victim to Allied bombing. Although transferred to new facilities, the production rate of the Ha-45 engine would never return to its previous levels.

As the wartime situation turned increasingly against the Japanese, efforts were made to introduce non-strategic materials into the construction of the *Hayate*. This resulted in the Ki-84-II, or *Hayate* Kai, which replaced portions of light allows previously used in the airframe structure with wood.

A further development of the *Hayate* was the Ki-84-III, intended for high-altitude operations and equipped with a turbo-supercharger. In the event, the Ki-84-III remained on the drawing board, as did a two-seater trainer version.

Production totals

Beginning in summer 1944, the *Hayate* was issued to front-line units of the IJA. By the time production came

to an end, a total of 3514 examples of the Ki-84 had been completed. Such was the demand for Ki-84 fighters that production was launched in underground factories to offer protection against bomber attack, and these were planned to provide an output of 200 aircraft per month.

Also included in the above production total were three Ki-106 prototypes of 1945, which employed an all-wooden construction and were made by the 1st Army Air Arsenal at Tachikawa. Although the Ki-106 showed promise in trials, by the time the war came to an end Tachikawa was still involved in weight-reduction efforts for the fighter. Also included within this total was the single Ki-116, built by Mansyu, and involving a standard Ki-84-Ia powered by a lighter-weight powerplant, the 1119kW (1500hp) Mitsubishi Ha-33 radial. Again, tests

were successful, but the war had ended before production could commence.

Once in combat, the Ki-84 found itself fighting rearguard actions against the Allies over the Philippines, the Ryukyu Islands and in the final defence of the Japanese home islands.

While the fighter demonstrated capabilities that made it more than a match for most of the Allied aircraft it encountered, it was plagued by production deficiencies as a result of inferior workmanship. Once in the field, the demands of fighting also took their toll and many aircraft fell victim to fuel pressure or hydraulic system failures.

End of the line
In the final effort to thwart the Allied bombing offensive mounted against the Japanese homeland, the Ki-84 was extensively used as a bomber interceptor. Ultimately, the *Hayate* proved to be the most effective

Ki-84-Ia
This *Hayate* was operated by the 58th Shimbutai in August 1944.

Japanese fighter during the last battles fought over Okinawa and the home islands. An example of the Ki-84 captured by the Allies was tested in the US after the war, where it demonstrated performance superior to both the P-47D Thunderbolt and the P-51D Mustang.

Kawasaki Ki-100

Developed as a wartime expedient to make use of surplus Ki-61-II airframes, the Ki-100 emerged as one of the most potent Japanese fighters of the Pacific War and showed such promise that it was soon ordered into production as a new-build aircraft.

While the Ki-61-II was planned as a high-altitude fighter to counter the US Army Air Force's B-29 raids that had begun in June 1944, its production was brought to an end in January 1945 after USAAF bombing raids on Akashi, where the fighter's Ha-140 inline piston engine had been manufactured. The loss of the engine source left a production total of 374 Ki-61-II aircraft, of which 275 were without engines.

Prior to the raid on Akashi it had been decided that the completed Ki-61-II aircraft should be re-engined and returned to service. With no alternative inline powerplants available, the Ki-61-II airframe was modified to accept a larger-diameter radial in the form of the Mitsubishi Ha-112-II, which offered the same power output as the Ha-140. Assistance in adapting the airframe for a radial engine was provided by examination of an imported Focke-Wulf Fw 190A, and further advice came from the Imperial Japanese Navy, whose Aichi D4Y3 featured a similar engine.

The re-engined aircraft was first flown in February 1945 and received the designation Kawasaki Ki-100. The aircraft quickly displayed excellent performance in the interceptor role, a capacity in which it was perhaps the most capable aircraft fielded by the Japanese during the war. Not

Ki-100-1a/b
Weight Maximum take-off: 3670kg (8091lb)
Dimensions Length: 8.80m (28ft 10.5in), Wingspan: 12.00m (39ft 4.5in), Height: 3.75m (12ft 3.5in)
Powerplant One 1119kW (1500hp) Mitsubishi Ha-45Ha-112-II radial piston engine
Speed 590km/h (367mph) at 10,000m (32,810ft)
Range 2000km (1243 miles)
Ceiling 10,670m (35,005ft)
Armament 2 x 12.7mm (0.5in) machine guns cannon, 2 x 20mm cannon plus two 250kg (551lb) bombs on underwing racks

only was the Ki-100 lighter than the Ki-61-II but it also possessed superior manoeuvrability and handling

Ki-100-la

This aircraft served with the 3rd Chutai, 18th Sentai, based at Kashina in spring 1945. This was the first unit to fly the Ki-100 in action in March 1945.

characteristics thanks to its lower wing and power loading.

Production begins

After the completion of three prototypes and successful pre-service trials, the Imperial Japanese Army immediately placed an order for the remaining 272 airframes to be fitted with Ha-112-II engines under the designation Army Type 5 Fighter Model 1A, or Ki-100-1a.

As well as making use of existing airframes, the Army called upon Kawasaki to launch production of a new-build aircraft as the Ki-100-Ib. Compared to the Ki-100-1a, the new-production version utilized the airframe that had been developed for the Ki-61-III. This featured a cut-down rear fuselage and all-round 'bubble' canopy.

A total of 99 Ki-100-Ib production aircraft were eventually completed

Ki-100-la

An aircraft of the 3rd Chutai, 59th Sentai. Chutai colours were blue for the 1st, red for the 2nd and yellow for the 3rd.

before production had to be halted in light of the increasing ferocity of USAAF aerial bombardment. Of these aircraft, only 12 had been delivered to operational units at the time of the Japanese surrender.

Ki-100-Ib

An unusual black finish adorns this Ki-100, operated by the 3rd Chutai, 59th Sentai. Note the cut-down fuselage of the Ki-100-Ib version.

CARRIER AIRCRAFT

At the outbreak of the Pacific War in late 1941, it was the Imperial Japanese Navy that led the world in terms of the employment of carrier air power. However, changing fortunes after mid-1942 meant that the IJN would struggle to adequately replace the 'first-generation' Aichi D3A, Mitsubishi A6M and Nakajima B5N aircraft with which they started the war.

This chapter includes the following aircraft:

- Aichi D1A 'Susie'
- Mitsubishi A5M 'Claude'
- Nakajima B5N 'Kate'
- Aichi D3A 'Val'
- Mitsubishi A6M *Reisen* 'Zeke'
- Yokosuka D4Y *Suisei* 'Judy'
- Nakajima B6N *Tenzan* 'Jill'
- Aichi B7A *Ryusei* 'Grace'

With a performance unmatched in 1941, the famed Mitsubishi Zero was the pre-eminent Imperial Japanese Navy fighter from the beginning of the Pacific conflict to the end.

Aichi D1A 'Susie'

Based on the design of the German Heinkel He 50, the D1A was a two-seat biplane dive-bomber that served on board Imperial Japanese Navy carriers in the 1930s. By the outbreak of World War II, most survivors had been relegated to service as trainers.

The D1A emerged in 1933 when a requirement was put out for a new carrier dive-bomber. Aichi's entrant for the 8-Shi requirement was based on the He 66, a single example of this export version of the He 50 having been imported to Japan and then reworked to meet the local specification.

Compared to the original German design, the new aircraft was powered by a Nakajima 2 Kai 1 radial engine and a second seat was added behind

---

D1A2

Weight Maximum take-off: 2610kg (5754lb)
Dimensions Length: 9.30m (30ft 6in), Wingspan: 11.40m (37ft 7.75in), Height: 3.41m (11ft 2.25in)
Powerplant One 544kW (730hp) Nakajima Hikari 1 radial piston engine
Speed 310km/h (193mph) at 3200m (10,500ft)
Range 930km (578 miles)
Ceiling 7000m (22,965ft)
Armament 3 x 7.7mm (0.303in) machine guns, and 1 x 250kg (551lb) and 2 x 30kg (66lb) bombs

---

the pilot's cockpit. Other changes included a strengthened undercarriage to deal with carrier landings. Further modifications were made during trials of what was then known as the Aichi Special Bomber. In late 1934 a production contract was awarded to Aichi after its design had fought off competition from rivals prepared by Nakajima and Yokosuka.

Into production

In its initial production form, the new aircraft was designated AB-9 by the manufacturer, while its official designation was Navy Type 94 Carrier Bomber or alternatively Aichi D1A1.

The D1A1 featured defensive armament in the form of two forward-firing and one flexible rear-firing 7.7mm (0.303in) machine guns. Typical offensive loads included two 30kg (66lb) bombs under the wings and a single 250kg (551lb) bomb under the

fuselage. Utilized during the Second Sino-Japanese War that began in 1937, the D1A1 had been withdrawn from first-line service by the time of the Japanese attack on Pearl Harbor.

The improved D1A2, designed in 1935, offered increased performance thanks to a more powerful Nakajima Hikari 1 radial, and also added undercarriage spats and revised windshields for the crew. As the Navy Type 96 Carrier Bomber, the D1A2 saw combat service during the Second Sino-Japanese War.

As of December 1941, a total of 61 D1A2s remained in service with second-line units, as a result of which the aircraft received the Allied reporting name 'Susie'.

In addition to the single prototype, based on the He 66, Aichi produced a total of 590 production aircraft, of which the majority (428) were completed to the improved D1A2 design.

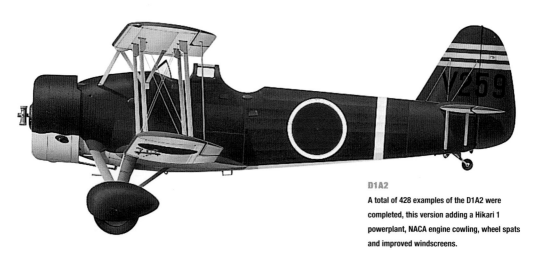

D1A2

A total of 428 examples of the D1A2 were completed, this version adding a Hikari 1 powerplant, NACA engine cowling, wheel spats and improved windscreens.

Mitsubishi A5M 'Claude'

Although only used in one major offensive during World War II, the A5M's place in history is ensured by its combat record against China and the fact that its appearance in service in early 1937 marked the emergence of the Imperial Japanese Navy as a modern force.

A Mitsubishi design was one of two fighters drafted to meet a 1932 requirement from the Navy that was intended to bring about self-sufficiency in regard to its aircraft equipment. In the event, Mitsubishi's entrant was judged unsatisfactory, and the Navy instead placed orders for the rival Nakajima A4N1. However, this fighter was always considered to be a stopgap until the availability of a more potent aircraft that would meet the 9-Shi specification issued in early 1934.

Exceeding expectations

The prototype of the Mitsubishi single-seat fighter designed to meet the requirements of 9-Shi received the manufacturer's designation Ka-14 and began initial flight tests on 4 February 1935. Although it suffered from some aerodynamic problems, the Ka-15 demonstrated an impressive

top speed of 451km/h (280mph). The second prototype addressed aerodynamic issues by replacing the original inverted gull wing with a new wing employing a straight centre section. After another four prototypes were completed, and various powerplants from Mitsubishi and Nakajma had been tested, the fighter was authorized for production as the Navy Type 96 Carrier Fighter, or A5M1. The engine selected for the initial

A5M1

Weight Loaded: 1500kg (3307lb)
Dimensions Length: 7.71m (25ft 3.5in), Wingspan: 11.0m (33ft 3.25in), Height: 3.20m (10ft 6in)
Powerplant One 436kW (585hp) Nakajima Kotobuki 2-Kai-1 radial piston engine
Speed 406km/h (252mph) at 2100m (6890ft)
Range unavailable
Ceiling unavailable
Armament 2 x 7.7mm (0.303in) machine guns

A5M2-ko

Operating from the carrier *Kaga* during operations off the coast of China in summer 1938, this A5M2-ko was camouflaged for operations over the Chinese mainland.

57

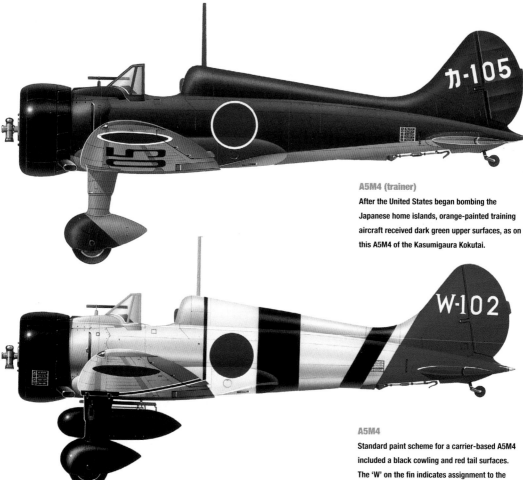

A5M4 (trainer)

After the United States began bombing the Japanese home islands, orange-painted training aircraft received dark green upper surfaces, as on this A5M4 of the Kasumigaura Kokutai.

A5M4

Standard paint scheme for a carrier-based A5M4 included a black cowling and red tail surfaces. The 'W' on the fin indicates assignment to the carrier *Soryu*.

production aircraft was the Nakajima Kotobuki 2 Kai 1, a nine-cylinder radial developing 433kW (580hp).

A prototype fighter based on the Ka-14 was ordered by the Japanese Army as the Ki-18. In the event, the Army judged the Kawasaki Ki-10-I biplane fighter to offer better manoeuvrability, and this promoted Mitsubishi to develop the Ki-33, an experimental fighter based on the Ki-18 but with an enclosed cockpit and a Nakajima Ha-1a engine. Ultimately, the Ki-33 lost out to the Nakajima Ki-27.

Meanwhile, the Navy's A5M1 was joined in service by the improved A5M2 in time to see combat in the course of the Second Sino-Japanese War that broke out in summer 1937. Compared to its predecessor, the A5M2, or Navy Type 96 Carrier Fighter Model 2-1, was powered by a Nakajima Kotobuki 2 Kai 3A engine.

Development of the fighter continued after the early models had gained air superiority over China. The A5M2B (Model 2-2) featured an enclosed cockpit and a Kotobuki 3

driving a three-blade propeller. Ultimately, the enclosed cockpit proved unpopular with pilots, and later A5M2B aircraft did away with this feature.

Cannon fighter

The A5M3a was powered by a Hispano-Suiza 12-cylinder liquid-cooled engine and armed with a 20mm cannon firing through the propeller hub. Since the Navy was unwilling to rely on a foreign supplier the next production model was the A5M4. This model was intended to improve the fighter's

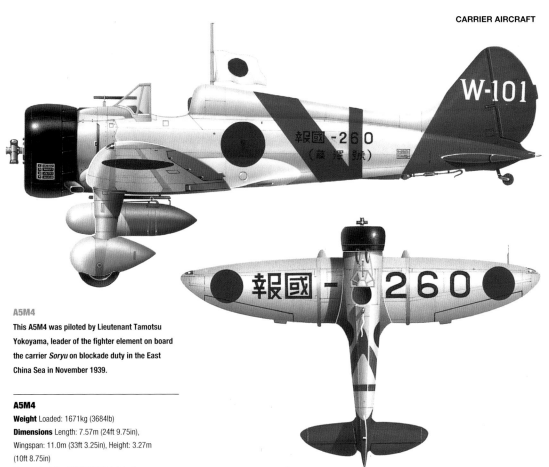

A5M4

This A5M4 was piloted by Lieutenant Tamotsu Yokoyama, leader of the fighter element on board the carrier *Soryu* on blockade duty in the East China Sea in November 1939.

A5M4

Weight Loaded: 1671kg (3684lb)

Dimensions Length: 7.57m (24ft 9.75in), Wingspan: 11.0m (33ft 3.25in), Height: 3.27m (10ft 8.75in)

Powerplant One 529kW (710hp) Nakajima Kotobuki 41 radial piston engine

Speed 440km/h (273mph) at 3000m (9840ft)

Range 1200km (746 miles)

Ceiling 9800m (32,150ft)

Armament 2 x 7.7mm (0.303in) machine guns plus 2 x 30kg (66lb) bombs

---

range, allowing them to reach Chinese fighters that had been withdrawn to airfields further from the front lines. Based on the late-model, open-cockpit A5M2B, the A5M4 was powered by a Kotobuki 41 and had provision for a 160-litre (35.2-Imp gal) fuel tank carried under the fuselage. Initially known as the Model 4 under the Navy's designation system, the A5M4 was later designated as the Model 24. The A5M4

entered combat against the Chinese in 1938 and was an immediate success. Ultimately, the A5M4 became the most numerous version of the fighter, with production being undertaken at Nagoya and Omura until 1940.

Ultimate A5M4

At the time of the devastating surprise attack by the Japanese on Pearl Harbor in December 1941, the A5M4 Model 24 had been joined in service by the improved A5M4 Model 34, which differed in its use of the Kotobuki 41 Kai engine as well as minor modifications to the airframe. However, by this time the aircraft was rapidly

disappearing from first-line formations, giving way to its celebrated successor, the Mitsubishi A6M2.

The A5M4 saw out its service as an advanced fighter trainer, and for this role a dedicated two-seat version was developed. The A5M4-K was produced via conversion of A5M4 Model 24 airframes, which received a simplified undercarriage, and two tandem open cockpits with prominent headrests. Development of the A5M4-K began in 1940, but by late 1942 these aircraft were being pressed into service for kamikaze attacks against Allied ships, together with the last remaining examples of the A5M4 fighter.

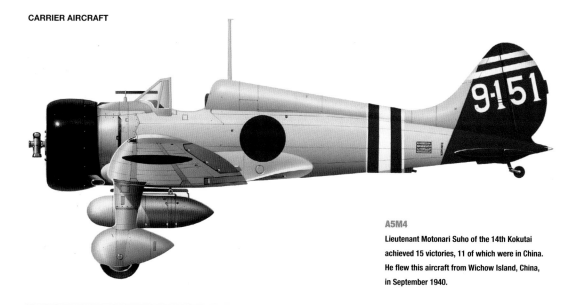

A5M4

Lieutenant Motonari Suho of the 14th Kokutai achieved 15 victories, 11 of which were in China. He flew this aircraft from Wichow Island, China, in September 1940.

Nakajima B5N 'Kate'

Responsible for delivering the hammer blow against the US Navy fleet at Pearl Harbor, the B5N was, at the time, the world's most advanced carrier-based torpedo-bomber. The 'Kate' remained a force to be reckoned with until it was replaced in 1944.

In 1932 Japan began to prepare a new series of carrier attack bombers, with development to be undertaken under the 7-Shi specification. After prototypes from Aichi, Mitsubishi and Nakajima were considered but all found wanting, the Navy put into production a stopgap design – the Yokosuka B4Y1. The next step towards the creation of the B5N was the 10-Shi specification of 1935, which led to the company's Type K design.

Type K

Nakajima flew a prototype of its Type K in January 1937, and the aircraft received the official designation B5N1. After experiencing some troubles relating to the hydraulic system, the prototype revealed performance in excess of the Navy's stated requirements, and the second

prototype – featuring manual rather than hydraulic wing-folding – was selected for production in late 1937 as the Navy Type 97 Carrier Attack Bomber Model 1.

After being re-designated as the Navy Type 97 Carrier Attack Bomber Model 11, the B5N1 was pressed into combat service over China, operating successfully from land bases. However, it was clear by now that changes needed to be made for the B5N to survive against more modern fighter opposition.

The next stage in the evolution of the B5N saw the aircraft fitted with a more powerful Nakajima Sakae 11 radial engine. Although developing 36 per cent more power than the original Nakajima Hikari 2, the new engine did not result in a significant improvement in maximum speed.

However, it did provide a greater margin of reliability, which was considered equally as important for long-range operations over water.

The re-engined aircraft was the B5N2, or Navy Type 97 Carrier Attack Bomber Model 12, and by the outbreak of the war in the Pacific this version has superseded the previous B5N1, as well

B5N2

Weight Maximum take-off: 4100kg (9039lb)

Dimensions Length: 10.30m (33ft 9.5in), Wingspan: 15.52m (50ft 11in), Height: 3.70m (12ft 1.5in)

Powerplant One 746kW (1000hp) Nakajima NK1B Sakae 11 radial piston engine

Speed 378km/h (235mph) maximum

Range 1990km (1237 miles)

Ceiling 8260m (27,100ft)

Armament 1 x 7.7mm (0.303in) machine gun plus bombload or torpedo of up to 800kg (1764lb)

as the interim B4Y1, among the Navy's
front-line units.

The B5N2's combat honours
include the sinking of three US Navy
carriers – USS *Lexington*, *Yorktown*
and *Hornet* – but by 1944 the aircraft
was obsolescent and was replaced
in its primary role by the Nakajima
B6N *Tenzan* torpedo-bomberr.

Second-line duties

Even after its replacement on carrier
decks, and after heavy losses had seen
it withdrawn from land-based bombing
operations, the 'Kate' still found a niche
in second-line operations. Among these
were maritime reconnaissance and
anti-submarine warfare, both of which
made use of the aircraft's impressive
endurance. The B5N2 was a useful
asset in protecting Japanese convoys
against submarine attack, and some
aircraft were eventually fitted with air-
to-surface vessel radar to aid them in
this role.

B5N2

This B5N2 of the 1st Koku Sentai,
1st Koku Kantai, was aboard *Akagi*
during the Pearl Harbor raid of
December 1941.

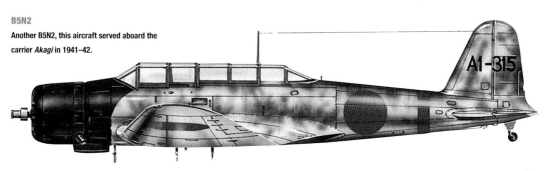

B5N2
Another B5N2, this aircraft served aboard the
carrier *Akagi* in 1941–42.

Aichi D3A 'Val'

An antiquated appearance belied the fact that the D3A was the most successful anti-shipping aircraft flown by the Axis powers in World War II. Even after the appearance of its replacement, the Yokosuka D4Y, the D3A soldiered on in land-based roles.

The D3A originated in the Navy's 11-Shi specification, which was issued in the summer of 1936, calling for a replacement for the Aichi D1A2 (Navy Type 96 Carrier Bomber) biplane carrier dive-bomber. Both Aichi and Nakajima were requested to design and build two prototypes each, while a proposal from Mitsubishi failed to reach the hardware stage of development.

Known in-house as the AM-17, the Aichi design incorporated a low-mounted monoplane wing inspired by that of the Heinkel He 70 and fixed

D3A1

Weight Loaded: 3650kg (8047lb)
Dimensions Length: 10.20m (33ft 5.25in), Wingspan: 14.37m (47ft 1.5in), Height: 3.85m (12ft 7.5in)
Powerplant One 895kW (1200hp) Mitsubishi Kinsei 44 radial piston engine
Speed 386km/h (240mph) maximum
Range 1470km (913 miles)
Ceiling 9300m (30,510ft)
Armament 3 x 7.7mm (0.303in) machine guns plus 1 x 250kg (551lb) and 2 x 60kg (132lb) bombs

undercarriage. The fuselage was of conventional circular section; overall construction was essentially all-metal. While the fixed, spatted landing gear harked back to earlier days in aviation, the Navy accepted this compromise because they thought the performance advantage offered by fully retractable undercarriage was not sufficient to warrant the additional weight and maintenance burden.

The prototype, powered by the same 529kW (710hp) Nakajima Hikari 1 nine-cylinder radial engine as found in the D1A2, took to the air for the first time in January 1938.

Initial flight trials revealed that the prototype AM-17 suffered from a lack of power and directional instability. These deficiencies were rectified in the second prototype, which as well as a 626kW (840hp) Mitsubishi Kinsei 3 14-cylinder radial featured increased tailfin area and a main wing of increased span and area. Strengthened dive brakes were also added in keeping with a revision to the specification

that now called for a diving speed of 444km/h (276mph), compared to the previous figure of 370km/h (230mph).

In this improved form, the aircraft, now designated D3A1, was selected for production as the Navy Type 99 Carrier Bomber Model 11, winning out against the rival Nakajima D3N1.

Production standard

Compared to the prototypes, the initial series-built D3A1 had slightly smaller wings and was powered by either the Mitsubishi Kinsei 43 or 44 engine, respectively developing 746kW (1000hp) or 895kW (1200hp). A prominent dorsal fin was installed to finally correct directional instability. Defensive armament was provided in the form of two forward-firing and one flexible rear-firing 7.7mm (0.303in) machine guns. In typical configuration, the offensive payload comprised a single 250kg

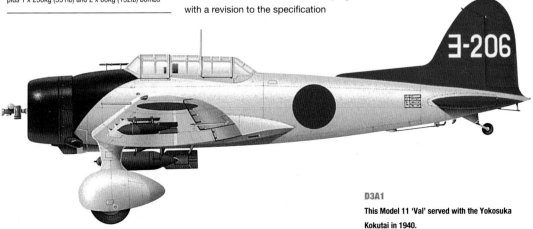

D3A1
This Model 11 'Val' served with the Yokosuka Kokutai in 1940.

(551lb) bomb carried under the fuselage, with the option of an additional two 60kg (132lb) bombs carried under each wing.

The D3A1 began carrier trials aboard the *Kaga* and *Akagi* in 1940 and the type undertook some limited combat operations from land bases during the months prior to the outbreak of World War II in the Pacific. For the first year of the conflict the D3A1 played a prominent role, beginning with the attack on Pearl Harbor in December 1941. The aircraft that received the Allied reporting name 'Val' was responsible for dropping the first bombs on US targets during the conflict, and a total of 126 D3A1s took part in the operation against US installations in Hawaii. Despite the loss

of 15 D3A1s, the raid succeeded in putting the battleships of the US Pacific Fleet out of action for six months.

In the Indian Ocean, the D3A1 successfully took part in the attacks that sunk the Royal Navy cruisers HMS *Cornwall* and *Dorsetshire* and the aircraft carrier *Hermes* in April 1942. However, the tide began to turn during and after the Battle of the Coral Sea of May 1942, when D3A1 losses began to mount. As a result, increasing numbers of the dive-bombers began to be reassigned to land-based units.

Improving the 'Val'

By June 1942 an improved version of the aircraft was available in the form of

the D3A2 Model 12. This was powered by a Kinsei 54 engine developing 969kW (1300hp). In an effort to improve the range of the aircraft, the D3A2 incorporated provision for increased fuel. Externally, the new aircraft differed from the D3A1 in its use of a longer and re-profiled cockpit canopy and the addition of a propeller spinner. Entering service in autumn 1942, the D3A2 was otherwise known as the Navy Type 99 Carrier Bomber Model 22.

Despite the appearance of the Yokosuka D4Y *Suisei*, the D3A's intended successor was not able to operate from the Navy's smaller aircraft carriers, which meant there was still a place for the D3A2 on the

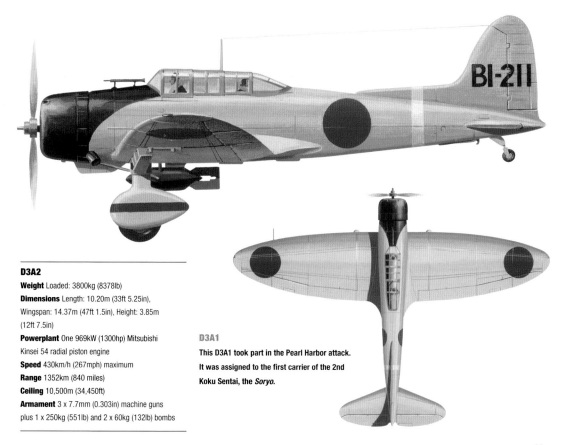

D3A2

Weight Loaded: 3800kg (8378lb)

Dimensions Length: 10.20m (33ft 5.25in), Wingspan: 14.37m (47ft 1.5in), Height: 3.85m (12ft 7.5in)

Powerplant One 969kW (1300hp) Mitsubishi Kinsei 54 radial piston engine

Speed 430km/h (267mph) maximum

Range 1352km (840 miles)

Ceiling 10,500m (34,450ft)

Armament 3 x 7.7mm (0.303in) machine guns plus 1 x 250kg (551lb) and 2 x 60kg (132lb) bombs

D3A1

This D3A1 took part in the Pearl Harbor attack. It was assigned to the first carrier of the 2nd Koku Sentai, the *Soryo*.

front line. However, the arrival of the much faster *Suisei* ensured that most D3A2s were relegated to land-based duties. The combat swansong for the 'Val' was during the fighting for the Philippines in 1944, when the dive-bomber sustained heavy losses to Allied fighters.

Training conversions

By this stage in the conflict, a number of D3A2 aircraft were being operated as trainers on the Japanese home islands. In this role, they served under the designation Navy Type 99 Bomber Trainer Model 12, or D3A2-K. Thereafter, the type returned to action as a kamikaze raider during the final months of the war.

Production totals for the D3A family amounted to 1495 aircraft in total, completed by Aichi in Nagoya and by Showa Hikoki Kogyo in Tokyo. The breakdown by variant comprised two prototypes, six pre-series D3A1s, 470 D3A1 Model 11 production aircraft, one prototype of the D3A2 and 815 D3A2 Model 22 production aircraft manufactured by Aichi, plus a further 201 D3A2 Model 22 production aircraft manufactured by Showa Hikoki Kogyo.

Compared to the D3A1, the D3A2 seen here was powered by a Kinsei 54 engine and featured a modified rear canopy and a propeller spinner.

JAPANESE CARRIER AIR GROUPS

The Imperial Japanese Navy, like the US Navy, stressed large-size air groups for their carrier force in order to best undertake operations in the expanses of the Pacific theatre. The force that attacked Pearl Harbor consisted of six carriers (the 1st Air Fleet) with their complements of aircraft boosted in number to reach a total of 430. The main aerial strike force was provided by B5N torpedo-bombers (also capable of delivering free-fall bombs), D3A dive-bombers and A6M fighters. By the time of the Battle of Midway in June 1942, the IJN was able to assemble a force in 'box' formation, led by the carrier *Hiryu* with 64 aircraft leading the port column, with the *Soryu* (another 64 aircraft, comprising B5Ns, D3As and A6Ms) only 3600m (11,811ft) astern. The other side of the defensive formation comprised the flagship *Akagi*, with the *Kaga* following behind. The Midway operation, intended to lure the US Pacific Fleet into a trap off Hawaii, ended in disaster for the Japanese, with all of the carriers involved being crippled by US Navy air power. With the loss of its 'big four' carriers, Japanese naval air power would from now on be on the back foot, despite the IJN being able to assemble a force of six carriers for the Philippines campaign in summer 1944.

D3A2

A late-model D3A2 (Model 22) of the Showa Hikoki Kogyo, representative of the aircraft's later land-based use.

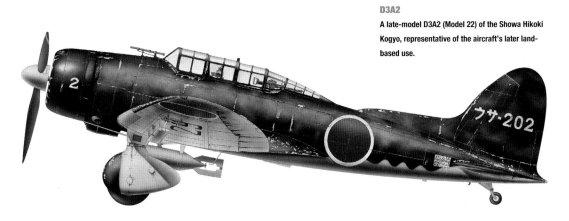

Mitsubishi A6M *Reisen* 'Zeke'

Inspiring respect from its adversaries, the A6M *Reisen* (Zero fighter) was the mainstay of the Imperial Japanese Navy's fighter arm throughout the war in the Pacific. In the process, the warplane amassed the highest production total of any Japanese aircraft in history.

The specification that eventually led to the development of the A6M *Reisen* was issued in May 1937 and called for a Navy Experimental 12-Shi Carrier Fighter. Both Mitsubishi and Nakajima were invited to respond with designs, with the aim of selecting an aircraft to replace the A5M (Navy Type 96 Carrier Fighter). Under designer Jiro Horikoski, Mitsubishi assigned highest priority to the development of the 12-Shi, in the process removing itself from

the Navy Experimental 11-Shi Carrier Bomber competition.

The demanding requirements for 12-Shi were revised in October 1937, based on the assessment of combat reports coming from China. With the demands of the project increased, Nakajima elected to withdraw from the competition, leaving Mitsubishi to go it alone with the design of its A6M1.

As originally drafted, the A6M1 was a low-wing monoplane of all-metal

construction, powered by a Mitsubishi Zusei 13 engine developing 582kW (780hp). Completed in March 1939, the first prototype A6M1 made its first flight on 1 April 1939 in the hands of test pilot Katsuzo Shima. The aircraft met or exceeded all requirements set out in the specification, and the only significant change during early tests was the replacement of the original two-blade propeller with a new three-blade unit. The definitive Nakajima

A6M2

This pre-series A6M2 saw combat trials against Chinese forces in the second half of 1940, serving with the 12th Rengo Kokutai in the Hankow region.

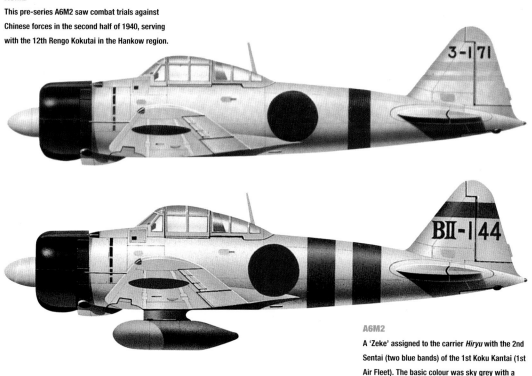

A6M2

A 'Zeke' assigned to the carrier *Hiryu* with the 2nd Sentai (two blue bands) of the 1st Koku Kantai (1st Air Fleet). The basic colour was sky grey with a matt black cowling.

NK1C Sakae 12 engine was then installed in the third prototype in late 1939, and in this form the Zero entered production as the A6M2.

By summer 1940 an initial pre-series batch of A6M2s had been issued for service trials, and in July that year a total of 15 aircraft were sent to China to begin combat trials. At the same time, the A6M2 was accepted for production as the Navy Type 0 Carrier Fighter Model 11.

Initial improvements

Modifications made to the basic design prior to the outbreak of the Pacific War yielded the Navy Type 0 Carrier Fighter Model 21. This incorporated changes including a reinforced rear wing spar and manually folding wingtips to fit carrier deck elevators. The Model 21

entered production with both Mitsubishi and Nakajima. From the 192nd aircraft, the Model 21 also featured a modified aileron tab balance.

Once the war in the Pacific began in December 1941 the Zero fighter rapidly gained air superiority, with standout performances in combat during the attack on Pearl Harbor, the Philippines, Wake, Darwin and Ceylon, and it played a vital role in a succession of Japanese military victories. While these campaigns were waged by carrier-based Zeros, their land-based counterparts saw success in the battles fought for the Philippines and the Dutch East Indies.

However, while the opening phase of the war in the Pacific had seen the Zero excel in an offensive role, after the Japanese advanced was halted at the

Battle of Midway the Mitsubishi fighters was forced to operate on the defensive, with diminishing results.

The next production version of the Zero was the A6M3, which had begun life prior to the Pacific War. This was powered by an 731kW (980hp) Sakae 21 radial engine equipped with a two-speed (as opposed to the previous single-speed) supercharger. The initial flight tests of the re-engined aircraft proved disappointing, however, and production was then delayed until a sufficient number of Sakae 21

A6M2

This *Reisen* was based at Rabaul, New Britain, with the 6th Kokutai in 1942. The basic grey colour has been improved with dark green blotches and a white outline has been added to the rising sun (Hinomaru).

A6M2

An overall dark green upper-surface camouflage was common among Imperial Japanese Navy aircraft later in the war. This A6M2 served with the 402nd Chutai of the 341st Kokutai at Clark Field, Manila.

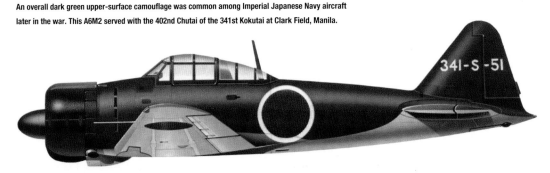

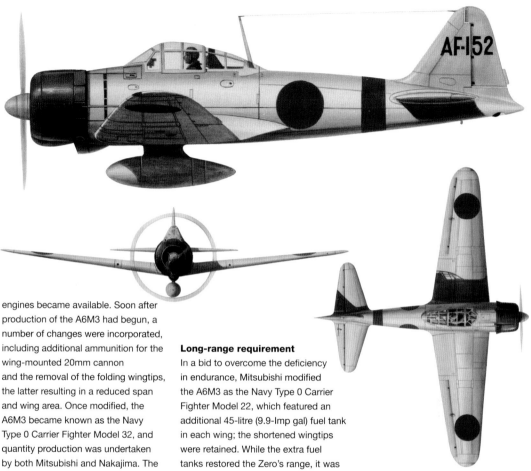

engines became available. Soon after production of the A6M3 had begun, a number of changes were incorporated, including additional ammunition for the wing-mounted 20mm cannon and the removal of the folding wingtips, the latter resulting in a reduced span and wing area. Once modified, the A6M3 became known as the Navy Type 0 Carrier Fighter Model 32, and quantity production was undertaken by both Mitsubishi and Nakajima. The square-wingtip Model 32 was briefly known to Allied intelligence by the reporting name 'Hap', later 'Hamp', before the previous name 'Zeke' was adopted as standard across all models.

Once thrown into combat from land bases during the Guadalcanal Campaign, the Model 32 began to reveal its shortcomings. Not only did the addition of the Sakae 21 engine require a reduction in internal fuel capacity but it also had the effect of increasing fuel consumption, in turn reducing combat range at a time when the fighter was being forced to operate from airfields far from the combat zone.

Long-range requirement

In a bid to overcome the deficiency in endurance, Mitsubishi modified the A6M3 as the Navy Type 0 Carrier Fighter Model 22, which featured an additional 45-litre (9.9-Imp gal) fuel tank in each wing; the shortened wingtips were retained. While the extra fuel tanks restored the Zero's range, it was now finding itself outclassed by new US fighters in the Pacific, including the P-38 Lightning and F4U Corsair.

A derivative of the Navy Type 0 Carrier Fighter Model 22 was the Model 22A (A6M3a), which differed in its adoption of long-barrel 20mm wing cannon. Meanwhile, a number of other A6M3s were tested in combat with 30mm cannon mounted in the wings.

Both Mitsubishi and the Navy continued their efforts to improve the Zero's combat potential, with a particular focus on high-altitude operations where it was thoroughly outclassed by the P-38 and F4U. One

A6M2

Flown by Juichiro Hanyo, this 1st Sentai, 1st Koku Kantai, aircraft flew from the carrier *Akagi* as part of the first wave of strikes against Pearl Harbor.

A6M2

Weight Maximum take-off: 2796kg (6164lb)
Dimensions Length: 9.06m (29ft 9in), Wingspan: 12.00m (39ft 4.5in), Height: 3.05m (10ft)
Powerplant One 708kW (950hp) Nakajima NK1C Sakae 12 radial piston engine
Speed 534km/h (332mph) at 4550m (14,930ft)
Range 1867km (1160 miles)
Ceiling 10,000m (32,810ft)
Armament 2 x 7.7mm (0.303in) machine guns and 2 x 20mm cannon

result of this was the A6M4, powered by a Sakae engine equipped with an experimental turbocharger. After teething troubles during testing it was decided not to pursue the turbocharged A6M4, and instead opt for the A6M5, which was intended to serve as an interim fighter pending the availability of the all-new Mitsubishi A7M *Reppu* (Hurricane).

Since the Reppu never entered production, manufacture of the A6M5 ultimately continued until Japan's defeat in August 1945.

Among the changes incorporated in the A6M5 were modifications intended to improve the fighter's speed in a dive. Work on this began in August 1943, when Mitsubishi modified the wing of an A6M3 for test purposes. The new wing was of reduced span and area and featured heavier-gauge skin and redesigned wingtips, again without folding. The basic armament of two 20mm cannon and two 7.7mm (0.303in) machine guns was retained, but in a further effort to increase performance,

REISEN PRODUCTION

Precise figures for the production totals of the Mitsubishi A6M will likely never be known, and currently published numbers are conflicting. However, according to most authoritative sources, manufacturing totals for the major production versions amount to 3879 aircraft completed by Mitsubishi and 6570 by Nakajima, for a grand total of 10,449 aircraft. However, these totals omit certain sub-variants, including the A6M2-N seaplane fighter (which is discussed separately) and the A6M2-K and A6M5-K trainer versions of the landplane. A total of 515 A6M2-K and A6M5-K aircraft were manufactured at Omura.

A6M2
This A6M2 of the 2nd Sentai of the 1st Koku Kantai is illustrated operating from the carrier *Hiryu* during the Battle of Midway in June 1942.

Colour scheme
The overall grey scheme worn by Imperial Japanese Navy fighters at the beginning of the war gave way to camouflage late in 1942. This initially consisted of over-painted irregular blotches of green and then with entirely green upper surfaces.

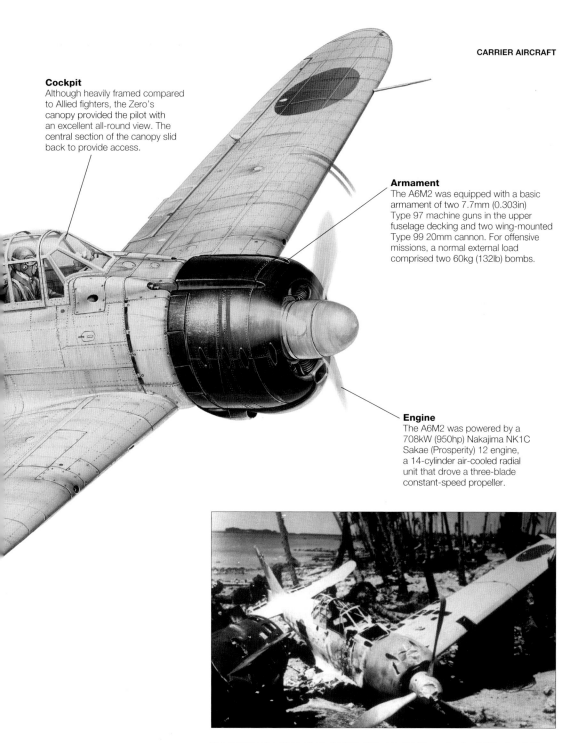

Cockpit
Although heavily framed compared to Allied fighters, the Zero's canopy provided the pilot with an excellent all-round view. The central section of the canopy slid back to provide access.

Armament
The A6M2 was equipped with a basic armament of two 7.7mm (0.303in) Type 97 machine guns in the upper fuselage decking and two wing-mounted Type 99 20mm cannon. For offensive missions, a normal external load comprised two 60kg (132lb) bombs.

Engine
The A6M2 was powered by a 708kW (950hp) Nakajima NK1C Sakae (Prosperity) 12 engine, a 14-cylinder air-cooled radial unit that drove a three-blade constant-speed propeller.

This wreckage of an A6M3 was one of 14 'Zekes' found by Allied forces abandoned at Munda airfield in the Central Solomons in August 1943.

A6M3

This A6M3 served on Kyushu, Japan, with the 251st Kokutai in late 1942. Note the 330-litre (72.6-Imp gal) centreline fuel tank.

new exhausts stacks were installed. The A6M5 also retained the Sakae 21 engine and made use of the additional wing tanks that had been introduced in the Model 22. Once in service, the A6M5 received the alternative designation Navy Type 0 Carrier Fighter Model 52. Unfortunately for the Navy, the A6M5 arrived in operational service in autumn 1943, only to meet the US Navy's newly issued F6F Hellcat, which proved to better armed and more resistant to battle damage.

The next Zero to enter production was the A6M5a, or Navy Type 0 Carrier Fighter Model 52A, which appeared in spring 1944. The skin of the wing now utilized an even heavier gauge for a further increase in diving speed. In terms of armament, the new version was 'up-gunned' with belt-fed 20mm cannon replacing the previous drum-fed weapons of the same calibre.

Otherwise known as the Navy Type 0 Carrier Fighter Model 52B, the A6M5b addressed the basic fighter's lack of armour protection. A sheet of armoured glass was installed behind the windshield and the fuel tanks were equipped with an automatic fire-

extinguishing system. At the same time, one of the fuselage-mounted 7.7mm machine guns gave way to a 13.2mm (0.51in) weapon.

In combat, the A6M5b enjoyed little success, serving as it did aboard the Navy's surviving carriers at the outset of the Battle of the Philippines. Here, the Zero and Japanese naval air power in general suffered a humiliating defeat to the US Navy in what became known as the 'Marianas Turkey Shoot'.

Beginning in October 1944 and the Allied landings at Leyte, the Zero began to be pressed increasingly into service as a kamikaze attack aircraft. For this purpose, the various A6M5 sub-variants could be equipped with a shackle for a single bomb in the position where the ventral drop tank was usually located. These suicide attacks began on 25 October, and a first mission saw the escort carrier USS *St Lo* (CVE 63) sunk by five Zeroes.

Lessons from battle

In an effort to wring some more performance out of the now-outdated *Reisen* design, the Navy requested that Mitsubishi modify the fighter yet again, this time drawing from conclusions learned in the Battle of the Philippines. As a result, the Navy's request of July 1944 called for a Zero fitted with two additional 13.2mm (0.51in) machine

A6M3

Weight Loaded: 2544kg (5609lb)
Dimensions Length: 9.06m (29ft 9in), Wingspan: 11.00m (36ft 1in), Height: 3.50m (11ft 6in)
Powerplant One 843kW (1130hp) Nakajima Sakae 21 radial piston engine
Speed 544km/h (338mph) at 6000m (19,685ft)
Range 2377km (1477 miles) maximum
Ceiling 11,050m (36,250ft)
Armament 2 x 7.7mm (0.303in) machine guns and 2 x 20mm cannon

guns in the wing, an armour plate behind the pilot's seat, an additional 140-litre (30.8-Imp gal) fuel tank installed behind the cockpit and wing racks for the carriage of unguided air-to-air rockets.

Since the revised fighter would be notably heavier than its forebears, the manufacturer sought to replace the Sakae engine with the more powerful Mitsubishi Kinsei. This was overruled by the Navy, and Mitsubishi pressed ahead with an aircraft that retained the Sakae 21, before the Sakae 31 with water-methanol injection became available. Flight trials of an initial prototype, modified from an A6M5, began in autumn 1944. After minor modification to the wing in the area of the gun bays, the resulting aircraft was approved for production as the Navy Type 0 Carrier Fighter Model 52C (A6M5c). Production of the A6M5c

The scene on board a 1st Koku Kantai carrier, as the Imperial Japanese Navy begins to launch its devastating raid against the US Navy's Pacific Fleet at Pearl Harbor, Hawaii, early on 7 December 1941. An A6M2 is seen preparing for take off, nearest to the camera.

was limited to just under 100 aircraft, however, since in November 1944 the next in the line of improved A6M5s became available.

The Navy Type 0 Carrier Fighter Model 53C (A6M6c) finally introduced

A6M5

This colourfully marked A6M5 served as an advanced trainer with the Genzan Kokutai at Wonsan, Korea. The ejector exhaust stacks were a feature of this variant.

the Sakae 31 with water-methanol injection for a further boost in performance. Manufacture was handled by Nakajima and the aircraft also featured self-sealing wing fuel tanks.

Dive-bomber

While a bomb-carrying ability had been introduced some time earlier, the Navy called for a dedicated attack version of the Zero, and this entered production in May 1945. In this, the Model 63 or

A6M5

Weight Loaded: 2733kg (6025lb)
Dimensions Length: 9.12m (29ft 11in), Wingspan: 11.00m (36ft 1in), Height: 3.50m (11ft 6in)
Powerplant One 731kW (980hp) Nakajima Sakae 21 radial piston engine
Speed 565km/h (351mph) at 6000m (19,685ft)
Range 1922km (1194 miles) maximum
Ceiling 11,740m (38,520ft)
Armament 2 x 7.7mm (0.303in) machine guns and 2 x 20mm cannon

A6M7, a more reliable bomb carrier was introduced with the aim of using this aircraft as a dive-bomber from smaller surviving carriers. Apart from the bomb rack, reinforced tailplane and provision for two 350-litre (77-Imp gal) drop tanks under the wing, the A6M7 was otherwise similar to the A6M6c.

After the A6M5c and A6M6c had both been found wanting in combat, the Navy finally decided to re-engine the *Reisen* with the Kinsei engine, as recommended by Mitsubishi. In November 1944 the Navy authorized production of two Kinsei-powered prototypes, spurred by the fact that Nakajima had concluded production of the Sakae engine. With an airframe similar to that of the A6M7, the resulting A6M8 eventually appeared in April 1945. The Kinsei engine was larger than the Sakae, requiring forward fuselage modifications, and the fuselage guns were deleted. Although assigned high priority, the Model 64, as the A6M8 was formally known, did not enter series production before the end of the war.

A6M6c

Weight Maximum take-off: 2950kg (6504lb)
Dimensions Length: 9.06m (29ft 9in), Wingspan: 11.00m (36ft 1in), Height: 3.50m (11ft 6in)
Powerplant One 843kW (1130hp) Nakajima Sakae 31 radial piston engine
Speed 557km/h (346mph) at 6000m (19,685ft)
Range 2896km (1800 miles) maximum
Ceiling 10,700m (35,105ft)
Armament 3 x 13.2mm (0.51in) machine guns and 2 x 20mm cannon

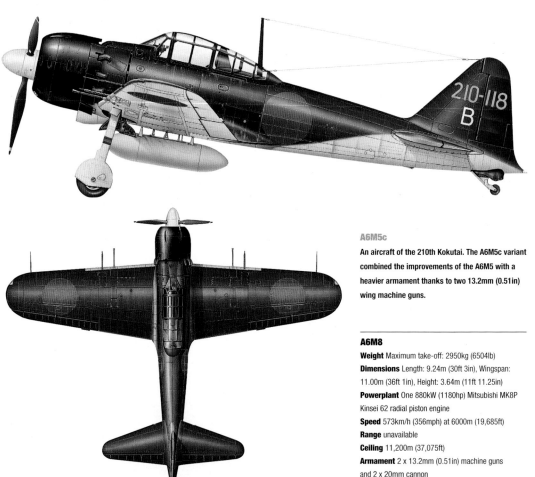

A6M5c

An aircraft of the 210th Kokutai. The A6M5c variant combined the improvements of the A6M5 with a heavier armament thanks to two 13.2mm (0.51in) wing machine guns.

A6M8

Weight Maximum take-off: 2950kg (6504lb)
Dimensions Length: 9.24m (30ft 3in), Wingspan: 11.00m (36ft 1in), Height: 3.64m (11ft 11.25in)
Powerplant One 880kW (1180hp) Mitsubishi MK8P Kinsei 62 radial piston engine
Speed 573km/h (356mph) at 6000m (19,685ft)
Range unavailable
Ceiling 11,200m (37,075ft)
Armament 2 x 13.2mm (0.51in) machine guns and 2 x 20mm cannon

Yokosuka D4Y *Suisei* 'Judy'

One of the fastest dive-bombers of the war, the D4Y *Suisei* (Comet) was a strongly European-influenced design but delays in its development saw it arrive in service in its intended role in March 1943, forcing the Navy to retain the antiquated Aichi D3A.

Incorporating all-metal construction and an aerodynamically refined airframe, the design of the D4Y was strongly influenced by the Heinkel He 118, an example of which was supplied by Germany to Japan in 1938. Smaller than the He 118, the D4Y was schemed to meet a Navy requirement for a carrier-based dive-bomber to replace the D3A. Compared to its predecessor, the D4Y was much smaller but carried a similar fuel load to guarantee a useful radius of action.

The initial prototype D4Y1 utilized a Daimler-Benz DB 600G engine, since the intended Aichi Atsuta liquid-cooled powerplant was not ready. A prototype completed the type's maiden flight in December 1940 and although initial test units with the German engine exhibited sparkling performance, they also developed cracks during dive-bomb trials.

The initial-production D4Y1 aircraft were powered by the Atsuta 12 engine and began to roll out of the factory in spring 1942. Such was the performance

advantage offered by the *Suisei* that the Navy requested it be adapted for the reconnaissance role as the D4Y1-C. In pre-production form, a camera-equipped D4Y1-C went aboard the carrier *Soryu* for the attack on Midway.

While small numbers of D4Y1-C aircraft were completed and served within reconnaissance detachments on carriers until the end of the war, development of the basic D4Y had continued, resulting in the dive-bomber version being declared fit for quantity production in March 1943.

Dive-bomber delayed

The dive-bomber D4Y added reinforced wings and improved dive brakes and was in large-scale service by the time of the Marianas campaign in June 1944. However, lacking fighter cover the D4Y suffered badly at the hands of US Navy fighters, and it became clear that the aircraft was lacking in terms of protection for the crew and fuel tank.

An improved D4Y2 became available in October 1944 and differed

in its use of a more powerful Atsuta 32 engine, while the D4Y2a introduced a rear-firing 13mm (0.51in) machine gun in place of the previous 7.92mm (0.312in) machine gun. When fitted with catapult equipment the aircraft became D4Y2 Kai and D4Y2a Kai, respectively. The final major production version was the D4Y3 with Mitsubishi MK8P radial engine, while the D4Y4 was a specialized suicide bomber.

D4Y2

Weight Maximum take-off: 4250kg (9370lb)
Dimensions Length: 10.22m (33ft 6.25in), Wingspan: 11.50m (37ft 8.75in), Height: 3.74m (12ft 3.25in)
Powerplant One 1044kW (1400hp) Aichi Atsuta 32 inline piston engine
Speed 550km/h (342mph) at 4750m (15,585ft)
Range 1465km (910 miles)
Ceiling 10,700m (35,105ft)
Armament 2 x 7.7mm (0.303in) machine guns, 1 x 7.92mm (0.31in) machine gun plus a bombload of up to 800kg (1764lb)

D4Y3
This *Suisei* was operated by the 601st Kokutai.
Later versions of the aircraft were equipped with
rocket-assisted take-off gear.

Nakajima B6N *Tenzan* 'Jill'

The B6N *Tenzan* (Heavenly Mountain) was Japan's standard carrier-based torpedo-bomber during the latter stages of the war. It was an evolution of the Nakajima B5N and was considerably heavier and more powerful than its illustrious forebear.

The B6N was designed to meet a 1939 Navy requirement and was externally very similar to the B5N that preceded it. The primary advance was the use of a new engine, the Nakajima Mamoru 11 radial providing some 80 per cent more power than the Sakae 11 unit used in the B5N. The first two prototypes of the B6N were ready to commence flight-testing in spring 1941.

A B6N torpedo-bomber swoops in low over the water to attack the US Navy aircraft carrier USS *Yorktown* (CV 10) off Truk in April 1944.

Teething troubles

Early development of the B6N was hampered by aerodynamic problems associated with the vertical tail and deficiencies exhibited by the Mamoru engine. Carrier acceptance trials finally began in late 1942 and revealed the need to modify the arrester hook. As a result the B6N was cleared for service in time to take part in the battle for the Marianas, but the aircraft's high landing speed and wing loading meant it was only able to operate from the Navy's larger carriers. The programme suffered a further setback when the Mamoru

B6N2

A 'Kate' seen in Imperial Japanese Navy service in 1944. The type was widely used in the late-war battles around Okinawa.

engine was removed from production, forcing a switch to the Mitsubishi MK4T Kasei 25. Adaptation to accommodate this engine – which had ironically been preferred by the Navy at the outset of the programme – proceeded smoothly, and the resulting production aircraft was the B6N2.

Total production amounted to 1268 B6Ns, and the definitive B6N2 in particular (1133 built) was especially active during the Okinawa Campaign, when it served both in the conventional attack role and in kamikaze missions on the US fleet.

B6N2

Weight Maximum take-off: 5650kg (12,456lb)

Dimensions Length: 10.87m (35ft 8in), Wingspan: 14.90m (48ft 10.5in), Height: 3.80m (12ft 5.5in)

Powerplant One 1380kW (1850hp) Mitsubishi MK4T Kasei 25 radial piston engine

Speed 480km/h (298mph) maximum

Range 3045km (1892 miles)

Ceiling 9040m (29,660ft)

Armament 2 x 7.7mm (0.303in) machine guns plus bombload or torpedo of up to 800kg (1764lb)

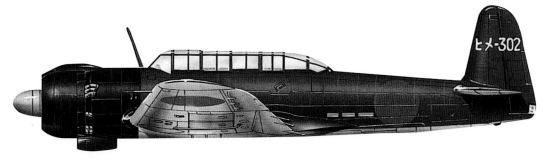

Aichi B7A *Ryusei* 'Grace'

A powerful carrier-based attack aircraft intended to fulfil both torpedo-bomber and dive-bomber roles, the B7A arrived too late in the war to serve aboard carriers and its limited production run was brought to an end by an earthquake as the conflict came to a close.

B7A2

The Yokosuka Kokutai was one of only two units to have operated the *Ryusei* in a front-line role, together with the 752nd Kokutai.

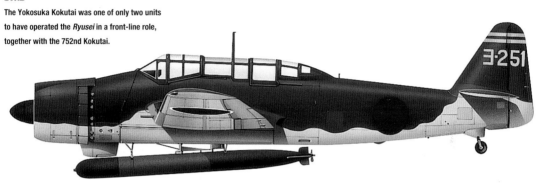

Development of the *Ryusei* (Shooting Star) was launched with the aim of replacing the Navy's Nakajima B6N torpedo-bomber and the Yokosuka D4Y dive-bomber. Although it was notably large for a Japanese carrier-based aircraft, the requirement called for manoeuvrability as good as that of the Mitsubishi A6M carrier fighter,

while carrying a weapons load of up to two 250kg (551lb) bombs or a single torpedo over a distance of at least 1000nm (1852km/1151 miles).

The design of the B7A allied a mid-wing configuration with a gull wing. The chosen engine was the powerful Nakajima Homare radial, which was intended to become a standard powerplant for Navy aircraft in the weight class of the *Ryusei*.

First prototype

An initial prototype B7A1 was completed in May 1942 and this aircraft was powered by what was then an experimental Homare 11 engine. Despite problems with it, the aircraft exhibited excellent performance and once an improved Homare 12 became available in April 1944 the B7A was approved for full-scale production.

Although it was considered easier to manufacture than its D4Y forebear, production of the B7A proceeded only slowly and was finally brought to an end when an earthquake struck the Funakata facility responsible for

AMBITIOUS REQUIREMENT

While the new class of carriers on which the B7A was intended to serve was never completed, the *Ryusei* nonetheless represented an ambitious specification from the Navy, and was one of the largest carrier aircraft completed for that service. Basic requirements called for the ability to carry two 250kg (551lb) or six 60kg (132lb) bombs internally, or one externally mounted torpedo; defensive armament of forward-firing 20mm cannon and a single flexible machine gun; a maximum speed of 569km/h (354mph); a standard range of 1000nm (1852km/1151 miles); and a maximum range of 1800nm (3334km/2071 miles).

B7A2

Weight Maximum take-off: 5625kg (12,401lb)

Dimensions Length: 11.49m (37ft 8.25in), Wingspan: 14.40m (47ft 3in), Height: 4.075m (13ft 4.5in)

Powerplant One 1361kW (1825hp) Nakajima Nk9C Homare 12 radial piston engine

Speed 565km/h (351mph) at 6550m (21,490ft)

Range 3040km (1889 miles)

Ceiling 11,250m (36,910ft)

Armament 2 x 20mm cannon, 1 x 13mm (0.51in) machine gun and 1 x 800kg (1764lb) torpedo

building the aircraft in May 1945. By that stage, the Navy had lost its carrier fleet anyway, and the 114 examples of the B7A that were competed instead served only from land bases.

The only production variant of the *Ryusei* was the B7A2 powered by the definitive Homare 12; this initially featured defensive armament of a single rear-firing 7.92mm (0.312in) machine gun, replaced by a 13mm (0.51in) machine gun on later production aircraft. A planned B7A3 with 1640kW (2200hp) Mitsubishi MK9A engine was never completed.

FLYING BOATS AND FLOATPLANES

As a nation of islands, Japan was already a long-term proponent of flying boats and floatplanes when the war in the Pacific broke out. As well as developing some of the most capable long-range reconnaissance flying boats, Japanese aeronautical industry also produced a range of float-equipped aircraft optimized for roles including fighter, surveillance and, uniquely, a submarine-launched attack floatplane, the Aichi M6A.

This chapter includes the following aircraft:

- Mitsubishi F1M 'Pete'
- Kawanishi H6K 'Mavis'
- Aichi E13A 'Jake'
- Kawanishi H8K 'Emily'
- Nakajima A6M2-N 'Rufe'
- Aichi M6A *Seiran*

One of the most impressive flying boats to see service during the war, the H8K was hampered by a lack of reliable air-surface vessel (ASV) radar. Here, US soldiers examine the wreckage of an HK8 on Makin Island, 1943.

Mitsubishi F1M 'Pete'

In terms of its design and the technology that it embodied, the F1M was a somewhat antiquated aircraft by the time war broke out, but it served well in a variety of roles in lesser theatres where it was able to operate unmolested by more modern Allied fighters.

In 1935 Mitsubishi designed the Ka-17 floatplane to meet the Imperial Japanese Navy's 10-Shi specification, which also attracted interest from Aichi and Kawanishi. The Mitsubishi offering was a two-seat, short-range observation aircraft with provision for catapult launch from warships.

Poor performance

As first flown in June 1936, the Ka-17 was powered by a 611kW (820hp) Nakajima Hikari 1 radial engine, but its performance was found to be below expectations. In particular, the aircraft was prone to 'porpoising' in the water and suffered from poor directional stability when airborne. The initial aircraft – built to the extent of four prototypes – received the IJN designation F1M1. The modified F1M2 represented an effort to overcome

the problems suffered by the Ka-17/F1M1 and introduced a more powerful engine in the shape of the Mitsubishi Zuisei 13 radial, as well as redesigned wings. Thus equipped, the F1M2 demonstrated improved performance such that it was ordered into production as the Navy Type 0 Observation Seaplane Model 11.

Wartime use

Once in front-line service, the F1M2 proved to be a reliable and versatile platform, turning its hand to roles that included ship-based observation, convoy escort, coastal patrol from shore bases and even fighter and dive-bomber missions. The ubiquity of the F1M2 was a reflection of the fact that it was the only observation seaplane of its class to be accepted for quantity production in Japan.

Derivatives of the basic model included the F1M2-K, which was converted for use as an advanced two-seat trainer.

Production of the floatplane known to the Allies as 'Pete' amounted to a total of 1118 aircraft, of which 528 were built by Mitsubishi and 590 by the 21st Naval Air Arsenal based at Sasebo.

F1M2

Weight Maximum take-off: 2550kg (5662lb)
Dimensions Length: 9.50m (31ft 2in), Wingspan: 11.00m (36ft 1in), Height: 4.00m (13ft 1.5in)
Powerplant One 652kW (875hp) Mitsubishi Zuisei 13 radial piston engine
Speed 370km/h (230mph) at 3440m (11,285ft)
Range 740km (460 miles)
Ceiling 9440m (30,970ft)
Armament 3 x 7.7mm (0.303in) machine guns and 2 x 60kg (132lb) bombs

---

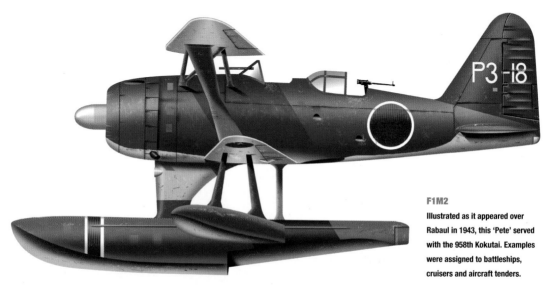

F1M2

Illustrated as it appeared over Rabaul in 1943, this 'Pete' served with the 958th Kokutai. Examples were assigned to battleships, cruisers and aircraft tenders.

Kawanishi H6K 'Mavis'

At the time of the attack on Pearl Harbor, the H6K flying boat was among the most capable aircraft available to the Japanese military. It remained in service until the end of the war on duties including maritime reconnaissance, bomber and transport.

Kawanishi developed its Type S to meet an early 1934 requirement of the Imperial Japanese Navy for a high-performance, long-range reconnaissance flying boat. Among the demands of the Navy Experimental 9-Shi Large Flying Boat specification were a cruising speed of 220km/h (137mph) and a range of 4500km (2795 miles).

The Type S completed its maiden flight in July 1936 and its design employed a parasol wing mounted on inverted-V struts over a slender two-step hull. In prototype form, the Type S was powered by four 626kW (840hp) Nakajima Hikari 2 radial engines that

were mounted on the leading edges of the wing.

In its initial form, the first prototype Type S revealed a number of shortcomings, in particular relating to its performance on the water. As a result, the hull was modified and the step moved back and this improved handling when both alighted and airborne. The initial armament comprised three flexible 7.7mm (0.303in) machine guns in an open bow position, dorsal turret and tail turret, while offensive stores could include two 800kg (1764lb) torpedoes or up to 1000kg (2205lb) of bombs carried on the parallel wing-supporting struts.

Improved prototypes

After trials, three of the four prototypes were retrofitted with more powerful 746kW (1000hp) Mitsubishi Kinsei 43 engines in a bid to further improve

performance. In this form, the aircraft were accepted by the Navy in early 1938, as the Navy Type 97 Flying Boat Model 1, or H6K1.

Meanwhile, quantity production was launched with these aircraft carrying the designation H6K2. By April 1940, the full designation of this aircraft had been revised to Navy Type 97 Flying Boat Model 11. Apart from minor equipment changes, the

H6K5

Weight Maximum take-off: 23,000kg (50,706lb)
Dimensions Length: 25.63m (84ft 1in), Wingspan: 40.00m (131ft 2.75in), Height: 6.27m (20ft 6.75in)
Powerplant Four 969kW (1300hp) Mitsubishi Kinsei 51 or 53 radial piston engines
Speed 385km/h (239mph) at 6000m (19,685ft)
Range 6775km (4210 miles)
Ceiling 9560m (31,365ft)
Armament 4 x 7.7mm (0.303in) machine guns, 1 x 20mm cannon plus 2 x 800kg (1764lb) torpedoes or up to 1000kg (2205lb) of bombs

H6K5

As long as it was able to operate unmolested by Allied fighters, the 'Mavis' proved to be a very useful long-range maritime patrol aircraft. This, the final production version, saw service until the end of the war.

TRANSPORT VERSIONS

The range and load-carrying capability of the 'Mavis' rendered it a useful transport aircraft, and it yielded a number of dedicated versions to fulfil this role. A pair of H6K2 initial-production models was completed to serve as VIP transports under the H6K3 designation. The major production version, the H6K4, spawned the H6K2-L, an unarmed transport that was otherwise similar. A total of 18 H6K2-Ls were supplied to Japan Air Lines, each equipped as 18-seat passenger transports. The H6K4-L was a similar unarmed transport, but benefited from Kinsei 46 engines and had additional cabin windows fitted.

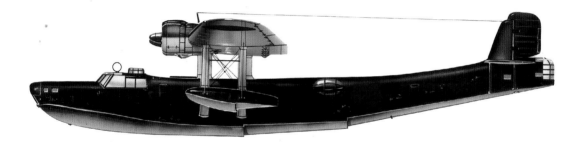

11 H6K2s were indistinguishable from the re-engined H6K1s.

The 'Mavis' entered service in January 1938 in time to see action during the Sino-Japanese War, and large-scale military service commenced with the outbreak of the war in the Pacific. However, the mid-1930s design of the aircraft began to see it increasingly withdrawn from front-line roles and from more hazardous theatres of action beginning in around late 1942.

Thereafter, the H6K was used for reconnaissance and transport missions in areas where reduced Allied fighter activity was expected. The 'Mavis' remained in service with the Navy until the end of the conflict.

A scene typical of the H6K's later service, and the type's increasing vulnerability, as a 'Mavis' goes up in flames, shot down by a US Navy PB4Y2 in the Central Pacific, 1944.

Extensive service

Ultimately, a total of 217 examples of the flying boat were completed in a succession of variants. Among the military versions, the H6K2 initial-production was followed by the H6K4, which became the most prolific member of the family; the full designation for this variant, which retained the Kinsei 43 engines, was Navy Type 97 Flying Boat Model 2-2.

The H6K4 introduced additional fuel capacity and revised armament: the original dorsal turret was removed and replaced with two beam blisters, each equipped with a single 7.7mm machine gun. Two further 7.7mm machine guns were fitted in the open bow position, while the tail turret received a 20mm cannon in place of the previous machine gun. Beginning in August 1941, the H6K4 also received 798kW (1070hp) Kinsei 46 engines, in the process becoming the Navy Type 97 Flying Boat Model 2-3.

In total, 127 examples of both H6K4 versions rolled out of the production facilities, and eventually they adopted the common designation Navy Type 97 Flying Boat Model 22.

The last of the 'Mavis' line was the H6K5, which was powered by Kinsei 51 or 53 engines and which had its armament revised once more, the open bow gun position giving way to a powered turret immediately aft of the flight deck with a single 7.7mm machine gun. The H6K5 as intended as a safeguard against delays to the Kawanishi H8K and replaced the Model 22 on the production lines until manufacture ceased with the delivery of the 36th H6K5 in 1942.

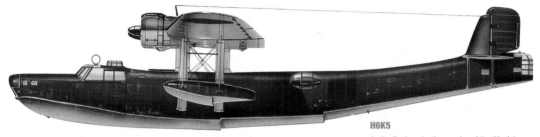

H6K5

As the final production version of the 'Mavis', the H6K5 introduced Kinsei 51 or 53 engines and revised armament.

Aichi E13A 'Jake'

The result of a protracted acquisition programme, the E13A was a reliable reconnaissance floatplane that served from the beginning of the war to its conclusion, and which became the most prolific Japanese aircraft in its class with almost 1500 examples built.

The Aichi E13A emerged as a further development of the same company's E12A two-seat reconnaissance seaplane design. Intended to meet a 1937 Imperial Japanese Navy specification (12-Shi) for a long-range reconnaissance floatplane, the aircraft was intended to provide escort to maritime convoys, which would frequently be operating beyond the reach of land-based maritime air

E13A1a

Weight Maximum take-off: 3640kg (8025lb)
Dimensions Length: 11.30m (37ft 0.75in), Wingspan: 14.50m (47ft 6.75in), Height: 7.40m (24ft 3.25in)
Powerplant One 805kW (1080hp) Mitsubishi Kinsei 43 radial piston engines
Speed 375km/h (233mph) at 2180m (7150ft)
Range 2090km (1299 miles)
Ceiling 8730m (28,640ft)
Armament 1 x 7.7mm (0.303in) machine gun plus up to 250kg (551lb) of bombs

power. In this role it would replace the Kawanishi E7K2 three-seat floatplane then in use.

At the outset, 12-Shi called for a two-seat design, and this attracted interest from Aichi, Kawanishi and Nakajima, each of which furnished a design: the E12A1, E12K1 and E12N1, respectively. Then, however, the Navy had a change of heart and instead launched a 12-Shi specification for a three-seat floatplane that would offer higher speed and increased range. These three designs would be the E13A1, E13K1 and E13N1. In the event, only Aichi proceeded with designs to fulfil both criteria, while Nakajima focused on the two-seater and Kawanishi on the three-seater.

The three-seat E13A1 prototype was completed at the end of 1938 and was a low-wing monoplane with a conventional tail unit, circular-section fuselage and twin-float landing gear.

with a folding mechanism so that the aircraft could be stowed on board warships. It was powered by a Kinsei 43 radial engine.

Competitive trials

The E13A1 was tested alongside the same company's E12A1 and demonstrated its superiority. Despite being larger and heavier than the E12A1, the E13A1 revealed superior stability and manoeuvrability.

Development of the two-seat E12A1 and E12N1 was then abandoned, and the prototype E13A was now flown against the rival Kawanishi E13K1 in service tests. The Aichi design was judged superior. As a result, it was ordered into production as the Navy Type 0 Reconnaissance Seaplane Model 1 (subsequently Model 11).

Initial production was handled by the manufacturer before it switched to Watanabe (later Kyushu). While Aichi

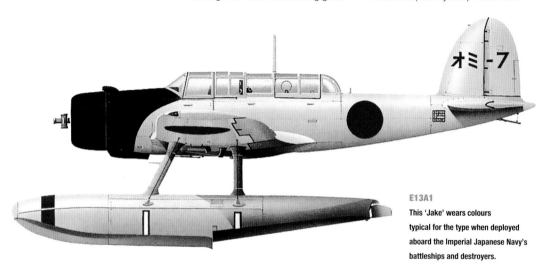

E13A1

This 'Jake' wears colours typical for the type when deployed aboard the Imperial Japanese Navy's battleships and destroyers.

completed 133 examples of the E13A1 by 1942 (including prototypes), in excess of 1100 were eventually built by Kyushu, as the former prime contractor was tasked to focus on the production of the D3A and D4Y carrier bombers. Further output was provided by the 11th Naval Air Arsenal, which manufactured around 50 examples at Hiro.

Into action

The aircraft, given the Allied reporting name 'Jake', entered service in late 1941 and the type was involved in reconnaissance patrols during the Japanese operations around Hawaii, flying from the cruisers *Tone*, *Chikuma* and *Kinugasa*. Prior to this, the E13A1 had seen its combat debut during attacks on the Canton-Hankow railway in December 1941, flying from seaplane tenders and cruisers to hit their targets.

In late 1944 a new version of the aircraft appeared. The E13A1a, or Navy Type 0 Reconnaissance Seaplane Model 11A, featured improved float-bracing struts with two additional pairs of inward-sloping struts, a propeller spinner and more comprehensive radio equipment. The similar E13A1b (Navy Type 0 Reconnaissance Seaplane Model 11B) was equipped with an air-surface vessel (ASV) radar. The antennas were accommodated in the wing leading edges and the sides of the rear fuselage.

The Kinsei 43 remained the standard powerplant for both the E13A1a and E13A1b. For night operations, both models could be equipped with flame dampers over the exhausts. In some aircraft, provision was added for one flexible downward-firing 20mm cannon, fitted in the belly of the fuselage, and optimized for use against US Navy Patrol Torpedo (PT) boats. A further

modification involved the addition of a magnetic anomaly detector (MAD) for use against submarines.

The E13A1 remained in service until the end of the war, its duties including operations from both ships and shore bases. The aircraft's impressive endurance of up to 15 hours made it ideal for long patrol sorties, and it also turned its hand to air-sea rescue, shipping attacks, staff transport and, as the war came to a close, kamikaze missions. Bombing runs could also be staged, providing there was little or no Allied fighter opposition.

The aircraft's deficiencies included limited defensive armament (one flexible rear-mounted 7.7mm/0.303in machine gun) and poor protection for the crew. However, its endurance made up for these limitations, and the aircraft was to be found operating wherever the IJN was in action.

Kawanishi H8K 'Emily'

Respected by Allied pilots on account of its formidable defensive armament, the H8K was completed in only relatively modest numbers, but saw service until the end of the war. It came to be regarded as probably the most capable aircraft of its type to see action.

Efforts to build a more capable successor to the H6K began in summer 1938, and a development contract for a large, four-engined flying boat was awarded to Kawanishi at the same time that the 'Mavis' was entering service. The specification to which the new aircraft would be designed was the Navy Experimental 13-Shi Large Flying Boat, which envisaged an aircraft that would be superior to the American Sikorsky XPBS-1 or the British Short Sunderland.

The prototype of the new flying boat, the H8K1, was first flown in December 1940 only weeks after Japan

had entered the Pacific War. The aircraft employed a high-wing monoplane configuration with a large conventional hull. Power was provided by four 1141kW (1530hp) Mitsubishi MK4A Kasei 11 engines.

The H8K1 provided accommodation for 10 crew and offered a good balance of defensive armament and protective armour. Among the self-protection features were partially self-sealing bulk fuel tanks within the hull, and a carbon dioxide fire-extinguishing system. The aircraft's impressive fuel capacity of some 17,040 litres (3,749 Imp gal) amounted to some 29 per cent of the

H8K2

Weight Maximum take-off: 32,500kg (71,650lb)

Dimensions Length: 28.13m (92ft 3.5in), Wingspan: 38.00m (124ft 8in), Height: 9.15m (30ft 0.25in)

Powerplant Four 1380kW (1850hp) Mitsubishi MK4Q Kasei 22 radial piston engines

Speed 465km/h (289mph) at 5000m (16,405ft)

Range 7150km (4443 miles)

Ceiling 8760m (27,740ft)

Armament 4 x 7.7mm (0.303in) machine guns, 5 x 20mm cannon plus up to 2000kg (4409lb) of bombs or depth charges, or 2 x 800kg (1764lb) torpedoes

maximum weight and ensured it would meets its envisaged range. In this initial form, defensive armament comprised single flexible 20mm cannon in the nose, dorsal and tail turrets, and in port and starboard beam blisters, plus single flexible 7.7mm (0.303in) machine guns in each of two side hatches and in a ventral position.

Early modifications

Initial flight trials involving the single prototype revealed that the H8K1 was dangerously unstable on water, with the aircraft showing a tendency to lose stability soon after the nose was lifted, in turn throwing water on to the

propellers and over the wing. As a result, the hull design had to be revised, with a modified planing hull and longitudinal steps on the forward part, before the Imperial Japanese Navy could order the aircraft into production in late 1941 under the designation Navy Type 2 Flying Boat Model 11. In the meantime, another two H6K1s had been completed as pre-series aircraft, incorporating the improvements that had been introduced on the modified first prototype.

While the aircraft's handling on water was still inferior to that of its forebear, it exhibited flying qualities and performance that were markedly improved over those of the H6K.

Although the first 14 production aircraft were all H8K1 aircraft, later examples replaced the MK4A Kasei 11 engines that were common to the prototypes with MK4B Kasei 12 units of the same power rating; the designation remained unchanged.

Compared to the first prototype the armament of the production H8K1 was somewhat reduced, with single 20mm cannon in the dorsal and tail turrets and four flexible 7.7mm machine guns.

First combat

The H8K1 entered service in time to join the fighting in early March 1942. The first mission flown was a night-time raid

H8K1

Attached to the Yokohama Naval Air Corps, the first prototype H8K1 was one of two that carried out a long-range bombing attack on Hawaii in March 1942.

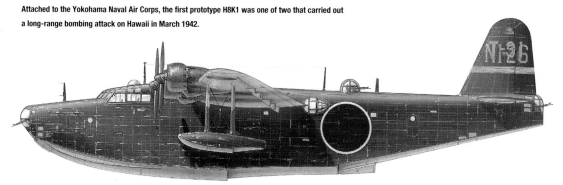

H8K2

An H8K2, or Model 12, of the 801st Kokutai, which was based at Yokohama. Despite its limited production run, the 'Emily' garnered an enviable reputation in service.

on Oahu Island, which involved taking off from the Marshall Islands before being refuelled by a submarine en route to the target.

The flying boat, which received the reporting name 'Emily' from the Allies, was used for wartime roles including bombing, reconnaissance and transport. While the results of early bombing raids using the H8K were somewhat disappointing, the aircraft excelled in the maritime reconnaissance role, thanks to its impressive defensive armament, armour protection and its high speed.

The major production version of the 'Emily' was the H8K2, with MK4Q engines, increased armament and fully protected fuel tanks. One other change related to the tail surfaces, which were slightly modified, and represented the only major external difference compared to the H8K1. In total, 112 examples of this definitive model were produced, under the designation Navy Type 2 Flying Boat Model 12. In this form, the 'Emily' had

defensive armament that was similar to that tested on the first prototype, with the addition of a single 7.7mm machine gun firing through hatches on each side of the flight deck. Appearing in service in late 1943, later examples of the H6K2 were provided with air-surface vessel (ASV) radar.

Transport versions

The first prototype H8K1 was reworked to create the H8K1-L, converted to use as a dedicated transport and now powered by 1380kW (1850hp) MK4Q Kasei 22 engines fitted with water injection. Passengers were carried on two decks in the expansive hull. This was followed by a production run of 36 examples of a production transport version, the H8K2-L, which provided accommodation for either 29 seated passengers or 64 troops, and featured reduced armament and fuel capacity.

The single H8K1-L served as a staff transport with the Navy Headquarters at Yokosuka, and the same design was

ordered into production as the Navy Type 2 Transport Flying Boat Model 32, and received the same Seiku (Clear Sky).

Two further variants of the flying boat failed to enter quantity production. These were the H8K3, which yielded two Kasei 22-powered prototypes equipped with retractable wing floats – intended to increase speed – and a retractable dorsal turret, but which were otherwise similar to the production H8K2. Another change embodied in the H8K3 was the replacement of the side gun blisters with sliding hatches, which were then incorporated on late-production H8K2 aircraft.

Finally, the H8K4 referred to the aforementioned H8K3 prototypes after they had been re-engined with 1361kW (1825hp) Mitsubishi MK4T-B Kasei 25b engines. In the event, the H8K4 and the planned H8K4-L transport were abandoned in order for Kawanishi to concentrate on fighter production for the defence of the homeland.

This example of the 'Emily' was captured by the US armed forces. The aircraft in question is of the major production version, the H8K2, formerly assigned to the Imperial Japanese Navy's 801st Kokutai.

Nakajima A6M2-N 'Rufe'

A development of the 'Zero', the A6M2-N represented the only truly successful floatplane fighter to enter service with any of the combatants during World War II. Although intended as a stopgap, the 'Rufe' was built in far greater numbers than its planned successor.

In 1940 the Imperial Japanese Navy launched a programme to field a new interceptor seaplane, the Kawanishi N1K1 Kyofu (Mighty Wind). However, it was clear that a stopgap fighter would be required before the Kyofu could be fielded. In February 1941 the Nakajima company was instructed to develop a float-equipped version of the Mitsubishi A6M2 naval fighter.

The need for a floatplane fighter was manifest in Japan's plans for an 'island-hopping' campaign in the Pacific that would involve occupation of small islands, many of which would not have airfields available to stage fighter cover. While aircraft carriers could provide some of the required air power, the Navy would have to call upon floatplane fighters to provide additional capacity.

Design of the A6M2-N involved taking a standard A6M2, from which the wheel landing gear was removed, and a large float mounted under the fuselage, carried on a forward-raked central

pylon and a pair of V-struts below the cockpit. A pair of cantilever stabilizing floats was mounted under the wings. The basic armament of the 'Zero' was retained unchanged.

First flight

The initial example of the A6M2-N took to the air on 7 December 1941 – the day of the attack on Pearl Harbor. The formal designation was Navy Type 2 Floatplane Fighter Model 11. Once in production, the aircraft was assigned the Allied reporting name 'Rufe'. Initial deliveries were made to the Yokohama Kokutai, and the aircraft were soon deployed to the Solomon Islands to support Japanese forces landed during the Battle of the Coral Sea. While most 'Rufes' deployed to the Solomons were lost to a US Navy air raid, those examples that fought in the Aleutians Campaign fared better.

In the closing stages of the war, the A6M2-N was used as a homeland defence interceptor, based on Lake

Biwa, and engaged in fighting over Central Honshu.

The final production tally for the 'Rufe' amounted to 327 examples before manufacture came to an end in the autumn of 1943. The aircraft's intended successor, the Kyofu, never arrived in service in significant numbers, with only 89 production aircraft completed until March 1944, by which time the strategic situation rendered the requirement for a floatplane fighter obsolete.

A6M2-N

Weight Maximum take-off: 2880kg (6349lb)

Dimensions Length: 10.10m (33ft 1.5in), Wingspan: 12.00m (39ft 4.5in), Height: 4.30m (14ft 1.25in)

Powerplant One 708kW (950hp) Nakajima NK1C Sakae 12 radial piston engine

Speed 435km/h (270mph) at 5000m (16,405ft)

Range 1781km (1107 miles)

Ceiling 10,000m (32,810ft)

Armament 2 x 7.7mm (0.303in) machine guns, 2 x 20mm cannon plus two 60kg (132lb) bombs

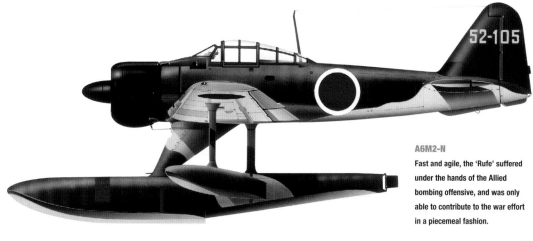

A6M2-N

Fast and agile, the 'Rufe' suffered under the hands of the Allied bombing offensive, and was only able to contribute to the war effort in a piecemeal fashion.

Aichi M6A *Seiran*

The *Seiran* (Mountain Haze) was the result of a unique requirement for a submarine-launched attack aircraft and as such the resulting M6A1 was the only aircraft of its type to have been built anywhere in the world. The end of the war prevented operational service.

The M6A *Seiran* was the result of an Imperial Japanese Navy specification of 1942 – Navy Experimental 17-Shi Special Attack Bomber – that called for a high-speed attack aircraft that could operate from the planned I-400 class of submarines, each of which had a displacement of 4572 tonnes (4500 tons). Although the end of the war precluded any operational missions being flown, the *Seiran* is assured its place in history as the only submarine-launched aircraft of World War II that had a primarily offensive tasking.

The envisaged mission of the I-400 and M6A combination involved the submarine taking best advantage of its 77,00km- (47,845 mile-) range to bring it within striking distance of the United States mainland. Once in position, the aircraft would be removed from its watertight hangar and launched by catapult. Each I-400 had the capacity to accommodate two *Seirans*.

In the event, only five examples of the I-400 submarine were laid down, but each of these had accommodation modified to allow the stowage of three *Seiran* aircraft, while the design of the aircraft itself was adapted to permit launch and recovery from floats.

Demanding requirement

As completed, the *Seiran* (which bore the in-house designation AM-24) was a conventional low-wing monoplane with twin floats each carried on a single wide strut. The main challenge for the Aichi design team was to produce an aircraft incorporating simple and robust folding mechanisms to allow stowage in the submarine hangar. Ultimately, this was refined such that a well-trained team of four technicians could ready an M6A for launch in only seven minutes.

The folding mechanism comprised wings that could be swung about their rear spar to lie flat alongside the fuselage, tailfin and rudder that could be folded to starboard and tailplane and elevators that could be folded downward. Areas of fluorescent paint were applied to the aircraft's moving areas to ease preparation for flight in the hours of darkness. In another innovative feature, the pilot could jettison the aircraft's floats shortly before launching an attack.

The initial prototype of the *Seiran*

M6A1

Weight Maximum take-off: 4445kg (9800lb)
Dimensions Length: 11.64m (38ft 2.25in),
Wingspan: 12.26m (40ft 2.75in), Height: 4.58m
(15ft 0.25in)
Powerplant One 1044kW (1400hp) Aichi
Atsuta 32 inverted inline piston engine
Speed 475km/h (295mph) at 5200m (17,060ft)
Range 1190km (739 miles)
Ceiling 9900m (32,480ft)
Armament 1 x 13mm (0.51in) machine gun
plus maximum bombload of 850kg (1874lb)

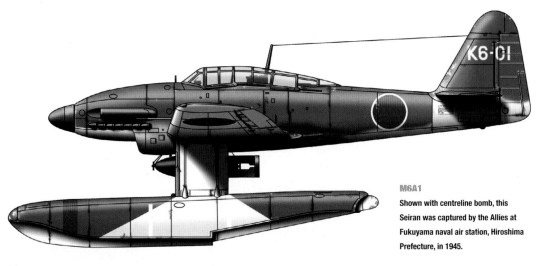

M6A1

Shown with centreline bomb, this Seiran was captured by the Allies at Fukuyama naval air station, Hiroshima Prefecture, in 1945.

Had it become available earlier, the Aichi M6A1 Navy Special Attack Bomber *Seiran* could have provided Japan with the ability to launch a strategic air strike with an impact comparable to the December 1941 raid against Pearl Harbor. In the event, the aircraft was only beginning to enter service when the Japanese government surrendered to the Allies.

appeared in late 1943. The aircraft was powered by a 1044kW (1400hp) Aichi AE1P Atsuta 30 inline engine. A total of eight prototypes were eventually completed, with all but the first being powered by the Atsuta 31 engine, providing a similar power output.

Series production amounted to just 18 aircraft, these differing in their use of an Atsuta 32 powerplant. Armament comprised one flexible rear-firing 13mm (0.51in) machine gun in an aft position, while offensive stores consisted of two 250kg (551lb) bombs, or one 800kg (1754lb) bomb or one 850kg (1874lb) bomb.

Initial plans called for the aircraft to be used in a daring raid against the lock gates of the Panama Canal. In this scenario, the Navy's 1st Submarine Flotilla would have entered combat with submarines I-400 and I-401, each carrying three M6A1s, and I-13 and

I-14, each of which carried two *Seiran*s. However, plans changed in late July 1945 when it was suggested that a number of these aircraft would go to sea with the 1st Submarine Flotilla to attack the US Navy's anchorage at Ulithi Atoll. However, the war had come to an end before any such raids could be launched.

Crew trainer

The only variant of the *Seiran* to be completed was the M6A1-K, a training version powered by the Atsuta 32 and equipped with conventional, inwards-retractable undercarriage for use by prospective M6A1 crew. Other changes included non-retractable tailfin and rudder. Only two examples of this version were built, and although initially referred to as the *Seiran* Kai, the aircraft was latterly known as the Nanzan (Southern Mountain).

I-400 class submarines

The Imperial Japanese Navy's I-400 class of submarines was drafted under the Fourth Reinforcement Programme, which initially included a request for a total of 18 such submarines, which were intended to provide a striking force with enough range to hit targets on the US West Coast. The I-400s – officially known by the designation Type STo, for Sen-Toku, or 'special submarine' – were very large submarines for their day, and their major innovation was the watertight hangar and, as originally planned, a catapult launcher arranged on the forward deck. Ultimately, the requirement for increased numbers of conventional submarines saw the I-400 numbers reduced to five. Of these, only three examples were completed, and the role of the offensive aircraft-carrying submarine soon waned. The similar I-13 class was similar in concept, but these boats were smaller.

ROCKET AND JET-POWERED AIRCRAFT

In common with Nazi Germany, Japan pursued a number of high-technology military aircraft projects that made use of the emerging technologies of rocket and jet propulsions. While the Mitsubishi J8M and Nakajima *Kikka* were essentially reverse-engineered versions of original German designs (the Messerschmitt Me 163 and Me 262, respectively), the radical Yokosuka MXY7, first flown in October 1944, was a uniquely Japanese solution, providing a piloted missile for the kamikaze mission in a vain attempt to change the course of the war.

This chapter includes the following aircraft:

- Yokosuka MXY7 *Ohka*
- Mitsubishi J8M *Shusui*
- Nakajima *Kikka*

Based on the Me 262, the *Kikka* (Orange Blossom) was somewhat smaller than the German design, due to the limited thrust of the available Japanese jet engines. Only one example took to the air before Japan's military defeat.

Yokosuka MXY7 *Ohka*

The desperation faced by the Japanese military by 1944 was such that it prompted work to begin on a special manned weapon designed exclusively for suicide bomb attacks as part of the Imperial Japanese Navy's wide-ranging kamikaze policy.

Known as *Ohka* (Cherry Blossom), the Yokosuka MXY7 is remembered as one of the most unusual weapons to have emerged from World War II. The origins of the *Ohka* lie in August 1944, when, in response to the adoption of the kamikaze suicide mission as an instrument of official strategy, the Imperial Japanese Navy launched work on a manned 'flying bomb'. In August 1944 the Naval Research and Development Centre began work

on what would become the *Ohka* – unofficially named 'Baka' or 'fool' by the Allies in the Pacific theatre. It is noteworthy that while Japan was also involved in developing guided missiles, none of these would become operational, and the problems of perfecting a reliable guidance system was sidestepped in the *Ohka* concept.

The Yokosuka-designed Navy Suicide Attacker *Ohka* Model 11 was intended to be air-launched

from a G4M2e Model 24J aircraft, a dedicated modification of the Mitsubishi 'Betty' bomber.

Air launch

The 'Betty' would bring the *Ohka* to within around 37km (23 miles) of its target, at which point it would be released and flown towards the objective by its own pilot, initially in a fast, unpowered glide. Thanks to its small size and speed, it was hoped that once on its run-in, the *Ohka* would present a difficult target for interception by enemy air defences. However, should the *Ohka* encounter enemy aircraft, there was little option for its pilot to take any more aggressive evasive action.

MXY7 Model 11

The first combat use of the *Ohka* was made by the 721st Kokutai in March 1945. A month later, the battleship USS *West Virginia* was damaged by *Ohkas*.

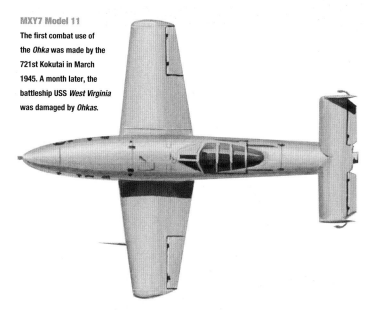

MXY7 Model 11

Weight Maximum take-off: 2140kg (4718lb)

Dimensions Length: 6.07m (19ft 10.75in), Wingspan: 5.12m (16ft 9.5in), Height: 1.16m (3ft 9.75in)

Powerplant Three Type 4 Model 20 solid-propellant rockets providing 800kg (1764lb) of thrust

Speed 649km/h (403mph) at 3500m (11,485ft)

Range 37km (23 miles)

Ceiling n/a

Armament 1 x 1200kg (2646lb) warhead

The 1200kg (2626lb) warhead in the nose of the *Ohka* would detonate on impact.

At a distance of around 4.8km (3 miles) from the target, the *Ohka* pilot would ignite the three solid-propellant rocket motors in the tail of the aircraft, and it would then accelerate to a speed of around 927km/h (576mph), now pulling into a steep dive. The warhead would detonate on impact with the target – typically a warship – killing the pilot in the process. Once the rockets had been fired, the *Ohka* presented a very difficult target for enemy air defences, and was essentially immune to enemy fighters.

Production

A total of 755 examples of the *Ohka* were built, some of these being completed as *Ohka* K-1 trainers. Another derivative was the *Ohka* Model 22, a reduced-size version for carriage by the Yokosuka P1Y1 Ginga bomber.

Around 50 of these weapons were completed, with a smaller warhead and a gas turbine engine. The Model 11 proved to be a failure, while another jet-propelled version, the *Ohka* Model 33, was not ready by the time the war ended.

The Model 33 retained the full-size warhead and was intended for launch from the Nakajima G8N1 Renzan bomber. Unrealized projects were the *Ohka* Model 43A with folding wings, and Model 43B with jettisonable wingtips.

A collection of *Ohka* piloted missiles captured by US forces at Yontan airfield, Okinawa. Although it had some early success, the *Ohka* was forever hampered by the vulnerability of its parent aircraft. *Ohkas* sunk the first Allied ship off Okinawa on 12 April 1945.

Mitsubishi J8M *Shusui*

Known as the *Shusui* (Swinging Sword), the J8M was a Japanese-built version of the German Messerschmitt Me 163 rocket interceptor, acquired in an effort to stem the tide of devastating US Army Air Force B-29 Superfortress bomber missions over Japan.

Informed by its local military attachés about Germany's development of the Messerschmitt Me 163B rocket interceptor, Japan was encouraged to acquire manufacturing rights for the aircraft and for its Walter rocket engine.

Me 163 copy

Efforts to import the required technology and documentation were frustrated by losses to Allied shipping, which meant that only a single engine and one Me 163 instruction manual reached Japan, where development was continued under the 19-Shi specification issued by the Imperial Japanese Navy. With these limited resources, it is all the more impressive that Japan managed to construct a functional copy of the Me 163B within the space of only a few months.

The task of designing and producing a Japanese version of the Me 163 was assigned to Mitsubishi, and while the Navy had issued the

original specification in July 1944, the programme was run as a joint Army-Navy effort, which yielded two separate designations: Ki-200 and J8M.

The design of the J8M1 prototype was finalized after official inspection of a mock-up in September 1944, after which construction of a full-scale glider version began at the 1st Naval Air Arsenal. The glider version of the aircraft, to be used for training, received the designation MXY8 *Akisuga* (Autumn Grass). A first flight, after being towed aloft by a Kyushu K10W1 trainer, was recorded in December 1944. Another glider version was completed as the Ku-13 *Shusui*. This introduced water ballast tanks to better replicate the weight of the powered aircraft.

Engine development

Meanwhile, development of the engine was carried out by Mitsubishi, in concert with the Army and Navy, and resulted in the Toko Ro.2 rocket motor.

The Ro.2 engine was first installed in the initial J8M1 Navy Experimental Rocket-Powered Interceptor Fighter *Shusui*, built by Mitsubishi. The J8M1 took to the air for the first time in July 1945, but the aircraft crashed when it suffered an engine failure soon after take-off.

No other examples of the powered J8M1 had flown by the time the war came to an end, and the MXY9 *Shuka* (Autumnal Fire) with a ducted-fan engine remained unfinished.

J8M1

Weight Loaded: 3885kg (8565lb)
Dimensions Length: 6.05m (19ft 10.25in), Wingspan: 9.50m (31ft 2in), Height: 2.70m (8ft 10in)
Powerplant One Toko Ro.2 liquid-fuelled rocket engine providing 1500kg (3307lb) of thrust
Speed 900km/h (559mph) at 10,000m (32,810ft)
Endurance 5 minutes 30 seconds (powered)
Ceiling 12,000m (39,370ft)
Armament 2 x 30mm cannon (J8M1) or 1 x 30mm cannon (J8M2, plus additional fuel)

J8M1

By the end of the war only one J8M1 had flown, but production was under way and at least seven prototypes had been built.

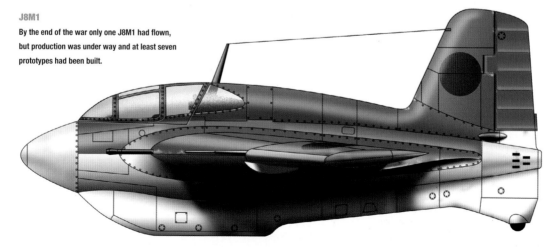

Nakajima *Kikka*

Inspired by the development in Germany of the Messerschmitt Me 262 fighter, Japan pursued a similar programme that resulted in the Nakajima *Kikka* (Orange Blossom), the country's only jet-powered aircraft to take to the air during World War II.

Kikka

A single *Kikka* prototype had been completed
by the time the programme was terminated,
although a quantity of pre-series aircraft
remained unfinished.

With its military attachés in Berlin providing optimistic reports on the progress of the Me 262, the Imperial Japanese Navy set about development of an equivalent aircraft. Work was to be carried out by Nakajima, with the aim of fielding a single-seat attack bomber capable of a speed of 695km/h (432mph) and a range of 204km (127 miles) while carrying a bombload of 500kg (1102lb).

Design of the jet fighter began in September 1944 with the project headed by designers Kazuo Ohno and Kenichi Matsumura. While the resulting aircraft was superficially similar to the Messerschmitt design, the Japanese machine was somewhat smaller as a result of the reduced thrust available from its indigenous engines.

Original plans called for a powerplant comprising two 200kg (441lb) thrust Tsu-11 ducted-flow engines. In initial prototype form, the Nakajima *Kikka* was powered by a pair of Tsu-12 turbojets, each developing a thrust of 340kg (750lb). These were soon replaced by Ne-20 axial-flow turbojets that produced a thrust of 475kg (1047lb) and which had been designed using photographs of the German BMW 003.

While the Ne-20 was more suitable than the Tsu-12, the aircraft still struggled to get off the ground and required rocket-assisted take-off (RATO) gear. Each RATO bottle provided 450kg (992lb) of thrust.

Inauspicious start

A first flight by the *Kikka* was recorded on 7 August 1945, with Lieutenant Commander Susumu Tanaoka at the controls. However, the aircraft's fourth flight had to be cut short on take-off from Kisarazu naval air station after Tanaoka discovered that the RATO gear had been incorrectly installed. The aircraft suffered some damage as a result.

As of 15 August 1945, when the programme was finally abandoned, a second *Kikka* prototype was under construction. A further 18 aircraft – both additional prototypes and pre-production machines – were also in varying stages of completion.

Un-built derivatives of the *Kikka* had been planned to undertake roles including reconnaissance, interception and training. For the latter, the third prototype was to be completed as a two-seater.

Kikka (first prototype)
Weight Maximum take-off: 4080kg (8995lb)
Dimensions Length: 8.13m (26ft 7.75in),
Wingspan: 10.00m (32ft 9.75in), Height: 2.95m
(9ft 8in)
Powerplant Two 475kg (1047lb) thrust Ne-20
axial-flow turbojets
Speed 697km/h (433mph) at 10,000m (32,810ft)
Range 940km (586 miles)
Ceiling 12,000m (39,370ft)
Armament 1 x 500kg (1100lb) bomb or 1 x 800kg
(1764lb) bomb

Types and Variants: Numbers Built

The following pages provide a variant-by-variant breakdown of all the Japanese aircraft featured in the previous chapters of this book, with a chronological listing of each version, and numbers built, as well as pertinent details of major production configurations. Thereafter, a table cross-references Allied reporting names for Japanese warplanes with the manufacturer's designations and designations applied by the Japanese military.

1: LAND-BASED BOMBERS AND RECONNAISSANCE AIRCRAFT

Mitsubishi G3M 'Nell' and 'Tina'

Ka-15: prototypes; 21 built, 1935–36.

G3M1 Model 11: production aircraft; 34 built, 1936–37. Powered by Mitsubishi Kinsei 3 engines.

G3M2 Model 21: production aircraft; 343 built, 1937–39. Powered by Mitsubishi Kinsei 41 or 42 engines; increased fuel capacity.

G3M2 Model 22: production aircraft; 238 built by Mitsubishi, 1939–41 and plus additional aircraft built by Nakajima, 1941–43.

G3M3 Model 23: production aircraft; built by Nakajima, 1941–43. Further uprated engines and improved armament. Total Nakajima production, 412 aircraft (G3M2 Model 22 and G3M3 Model 23).

Note also that G3M1-L and L3Y1 Model 11 transport aircraft were converted from G3M1 aircraft, while L3Y2 Model 12 transports were converted from G3M2 Model 21 aircraft.

Production of the G3M bomber was undertaken by both the original manufacturer Mitsubishi and by Nakajima. In common with most frontline Japanese types of the Pacific War, the 'Nell' underwent several different updates, with the final production model being built exclusively by Nakajima, leaving Mitsubishi to focus on its designated successor, the G4M.

Mitsubishi Ki-15 and C5M 'Babs'

Ki-15-I, Ki-15-II and Ki-15-III: production aircraft, 439 built, 1936–40. Ki-15-I was initial production version for Imperial Japanese Army, with Nakajima Ha-8 engine. Ki-15-II introduced the Mitsubishi Ha-26-I engine, while the Ki-15-III model introduced a Mitsubishi 102 engine but did not see quantity production.

C5M1: production aircraft for Imperial Japanese Navy; 20 built, 1938. Equivalent to Ki-15-II.

C5M2: production aircraft for Imperial Japanese Navy; 30 built, 1940. Powered by Nakajima Sakae 12 engine.

Mitsubishi Ki-21 'Sally'

Ki-21: prototypes and service trials aircraft; eight built, 1936–38. Nakajima Ha-5 engines.

Ki-21-Ia: production aircraft; 143 built, 1938–39.

Ki-21-Ib: production aircraft; 120 built, 1939–40. Improved defensive armament and enlarged bomb bay.

Ki-21-Ic: production aircraft; 160 built, 1940. Increased fuel capacity and further improved defensive armament.

Ki-21-II: service trials aircraft; four built, 1940. Introduced Mitsubishi Ha-101 engines.

Ki-21-IIa: production aircraft; 590 built, 1940–42. Retained armament of the Ki-21-Ic:

Ki-21-IIb: production aircraft; 688 built, 1942–44. Generally similar to Ki-21-IIa but with minor refinements.

Nakajima production accounted for an additional 351 Ki-21-Ia, Ki-21-Ib and Ki-21-Ic production aircraft built 1938–41.

MC-21: Ki-21-I aircraft modified as unarmed transports.

Mitsubishi Ki-30 'Ann'

Ki-30: prototypes; two built, 1937.

Ki-30: service trials aircraft; 16 built, 1937–38.

Ki-30: production aircraft; 618 built by Mitsubishi, 1938–40, and 68 built by Tachikawa, 1939–41.

Mitsubishi Ki-51 'Sonia'
Ki-51: prototypes; two built, 1939.
Ki-51: service trials aircraft; 11 built, 1939.
Ki-51: pre-production aircraft; 1459 built by Mitsubishi, 1940–44, and 913 built by Tachikawa, 1941–45. One example converted as a Ki-51a prototype for tactical reconnaissance.
Ki-71: prototypes; three built by Tachikawa. Reconnaissance.

Kawasaki Ki-48 'Lily'
Ki-48: prototypes; four built, 1939.
Ki-48: pre-production aircraft; five built, 1940.
Ki-48-I: initial production aircraft; 557 built, 1940–42. Of these, some aircraft completed as Ki-48-Ib with minor equipment changes and detail refinements; earlier aircraft retrospectively designated Ki-48-Ia.
Ki-48-II: prototypes; three built, 1942. Protected fuel tanks, armour protection and Nakajima Ha-115 engines.
Ki-48-II: production aircraft; 1408 built, 1942–44. Of these, Ki-48-IIa featured defensive armament of Ki-48-Ia but increased bombload; Ki-48-IIb version generally as Ki-48-Ia but with dive brakes added.
   Unbuilt versions comprised Ki-81 with heavier armour and armament and Ki-174 single-seat special attack version of Ki-48.

Nakajima Ki-49 *Donryu* 'Helen'
Ki-49: initial prototypes; three built, 1939. Nakajima Ha-5 Kai or Ha-41 engines.
Ki-49: pre-production aircraft; seven built, 1940.
Ki-49-I: production aircraft; 129 built, 1941–42. Nakajima Ha-41 engines.
Ki-49-II: prototypes; two built, 1942. Nakajima Ha-109 engines, improved armour, self-sealing fuel tanks.
Ki-49-II: production aircraft; 617 built by Nakajima, 1942–44, 50 built by Tachikawa, 1943–44. These were completed either as the Ki-49-IIa that retained the armament of the Ki-49-I, or the Ki-49-IIb that introduced revised armament.
Ki-49-III: prototypes; six built, 1943. Nakajima Ha-117 engines.
Ki-58: escort fighter prototypes; three built, 1940–41. Nakajima Ha-117 engines.
Ki-80: pathfinder prototypes; two built, 1941.

Mitsubishi Ki-46 'Dinah'
Ki-46 and Ki-46-I: prototypes and pre-production aircraft; 34 built, 1939–40. Mitsubishi Ha-21-I engines.
Ki-46-II: production aircraft; 1093 built, 1940–44. Mitsubishi Ha-102 engines. Some of these aircraft converted to three-seat radio/navigation trainers as Ki-46-II Kai.
Ki-46-III: prototypes; two built, 1942.
Ki-46-III: production aircraft; 609 built, 1942–45. Some of these aircraft converted to fighter interceptors as Ki-46-III Kai, or ground-attack aircraft as Ki-46-IIIb.
Ki-46-IV: prototypes; four built, 1943–44. Mitsubishi Ha-112-II Ru engines.

Mitsubishi G4M 'Betty'
12-Shi: initial prototypes; two built, 1939–40. Mitsubishi Kasei 11 engines.
G6M1: production heavy escort fighter; 30 built, 1940. Some of these later converted as G6M1-K trainers or G6M1-L2 transports.
G4M1: production aircraft; 1200 built, 1941–44. Initial sub-variant was G4M1 Model 11, followed by the generally similar G4M1 Model 12.
G4M2: production aircraft; 1154 built, 1942–45. Completed as G4M2 Model 22A and G4M2 Model 22B sub-variants that were both powered by Mitsubishi MK4P Kasei engines but differed in terms of armament. They were followed by G4M2a Model 24 with Mitsubishi MK4T Kasei engines and bulged bomb bay doors; the G4M2a Model 24A/24B sub-variants differed in terms of armament. G4M2e Model 24J sub-variant had equipment for launching the Ohka piloted missile.
G4M3: final production aircraft; 60 built, 1943–45. Completed as Model 34, with self-sealing tanks, improved armour protection.
   Notable experimental variants included G4M2b Model 25, G4M2c Model 26, G4M2d Model 26 and G4M3 Model 36, all of which completed in only small numbers for evaluation.

Imperial Japanese Navy personnel load a torpedo on to a G4M1 bomber. A total of 1200 examples of this version of the 'Betty' were completed during 1941–44. Sub-variants comprised the G4M1 Model 11, and the generally similar G4M1 Model 12.

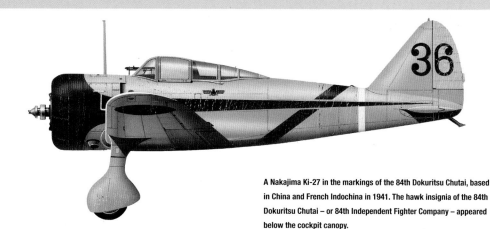

A Nakajima Ki-27 in the markings of the 84th Dokuritsu Chutai, based in China and French Indochina in 1941. The hawk insignia of the 84th Dokuritsu Chutai – or 84th Independent Fighter Company – appeared below the cockpit canopy.

Mitsubishi Ki-67 *Hiryu* 'Peggy'

Ki-67: prototypes and production aircraft; 606 built by Mitsubishi, 91 built by Kawasaki, and one built by Tachikawa. Of the Mitsubishi total, 29 were assembled by Nippon Kokusai. In addition to the standard Ki-67-I production aircraft, and included in the above total, the Ki-67-I Kai designation applied to aircraft converted for the kamikaze role, while the Ki-109 was a heavy fighter variant (22 built).

2: LAND-BASED FIGHTERS

Nakajima Ki-27 'Nate'

P.E.: initial prototype; one built, 1936.

Ki-27: prototype; two built, 1936.

Ki-27: pre-production aircraft; 10 built, 1937.

Ki-27a and Ki-27b: production aircraft; 2005 built by Nakajima, 1937–42, including training versions, and 1379 built by Mansyu Hikoki Seizo. Later-production Ki-27b was slightly improved compared to Ki-27a.

Ki-27 Kai: lightweight experimental fighter prototype; two built, 1940.

Nakajima Ki-43 *Hayabusa* 'Oscar'

Ki-43: initial prototypes; three built, 1938–39. Nakajima Sakae Ha-25 engine.

Ki-43: service trials aircraft; 10 built, 1939–40.

Ki-43-I: initial production aircraft; 716 built by Nakajima, 1941–43. Sub-variants designated Ki-43-Ia, Ki-43-Ib and Ki-43-Ic featured slight differences in terms of armament.

Ki-43-II: prototypes; five built, 1942. Introduced self-sealing tanks, armour and Nakajima Ha-115 engine.

Ki-43-II: service trials aircraft; three built, 1942.

Ki-43-II: initial second-generation production aircraft; 2491 built by Nakajima, 1942–1944. Sub-variants comprised Ki-43-IIa with armament as Ki-43-Ic plus underwing bomb racks, and generally similar Ki-43-IIb with minor equipment changes. Ki-43-II Kai version incorporated progressive modifications of Ki-43-IIa and Ki-43-IIb.

Ki-43-IIa: production aircraft; 49 built by Tachikawa, 1942–43. As above.

Ki-43-IIIa: prototypes; 10 built, 1944–45. Generally as Ki-43-II Kai but with Nakajima Ha-115-II engine.

Ki-43-II and Ki-43-IIIa: production aircraft; 2,629 built by Tachikawa, 1943–1945.

Ki-43-IIIb: interceptor prototypes; two built by Tachikawa, 1945. Mitsubishi Ha-112 engine and underwing racks, as on Ki-43-IIa.

Nakajima Ki-44 *Shoki* 'Tojo'

Ki-44: initial prototypes; three built, 1940–41. Nakajima Ha-41 engine.

Ki-44: pre-production aircraft; seven built, 1941.

Ki-44-I: production aircraft; 40 built, 1942. Initial production Ki-44-Ia version generally similar to Ki-44. Ki-44-Ib as for Ki-44-Ia but with improved armament. Ki-44-Ic as for Ki-44-Ib but with modified undercarriage.

Ki-44-II: prototypes; five built, 1942. Nakajima Ha-109 engine.

Ki-44-II: pre-production aircraft; three built, 1942.

Ki-44-II and Ki-44-III: production aircraft; 1167 built, 1942–44. Initial production Ki-44-IIa version retained armament of the Ki-44-Ia.

Ki-44-IIb was major production version with armament as Ki-44-Ib.

Ki-44-IIc introduced new armament.

Ki-44-IIIa introduced Nakajima Ha-145 engine and revised armament.

Ki-44-IIIb was final production version, but with further revised armament.

Kawasaki Ki-45 *Toryu* 'Nick'

Ki-45: initial prototypes; three aircraft built, 1939. Nakajima Ha-20B engines.

Ki-45 Improved Type 1: additional prototypes; eight aircraft built, 1940–41. Nakajima Ha-25 engines.

Ki-45 Kai: additional prototypes; three aircraft built, 1941. Nakajima Ha-25 engines.

Ki-45 Kai: pre-production aircraft; 12 aircraft built, 1941.

Ki-45 Kai-a and Kai-b: production aircraft; 305 built by Kawasaki, 1942–43, 893 built by Akashi (Kai-a, Kai-b, and Kai-d), 1942–45. Kai-a was the initial production aircraft with Nakajima Ha-25 engines. Kai-b was ground-attack version with Mitsubishi Ha-102 engines, Kai-c was a night-fighter with Ha-102 engines, while Kai-d was an anti-shipping version with Ha-102 engines.

Ki-45 Kai-c: production aircraft; 477 built by Akashi, 1944.

Ki-45-II: proposed version powered by Mitsubishi Ha-112-II engines, in the event Kawasaki instead developed Ki-96; single-seat fighter, prototype only.

Nakajima J1N *Gekko* 'Irving'

J1N: initial prototypes; two built, 1941.

J1N1-C: prototypes; seven built, 1941–42. Long-range reconnaissance version.

J1N1-C long-range reconnaissance aircraft, J1N1-R (revised designation for J1N1-C), J1N1-F with revised armament, J1N1-C Kai night-fighter conversion, J1N1-S night-fighter production aircraft, and J1N1-Sa night-fighter with revised armament: production aircraft; 470 built, 1942–44.

Kawasaki Ki-61 *Hien* 'Tony'

Ki-61: initial prototypes; 12 built; 1941–42.

Ki-61-I: initial production aircraft; 1380 built; 1942–44. Ki-61-

Ia as Ki-61-I but with revised armament; further armament variations introduced in the Ki-61-Ib, Ki-61-Ic and Ki-61-Id.

Ki-61-I Kai: production aircraft; 1274 built; 1944–45.

Ki-61-II: prototypes; eight built; 1943–44. Increased-area wing and Kawasaki Ha-140 engine.

Ki-61-II Kai: prototypes and pre-production aircraft; 30 built; 1944. Reversion to Ki-61-I wing, redesigned tail surfaces.

Ki-61-II Kai: production aircraft; 374 built; 1944–45. Of these, 275 were completed as Ki-100s (see below). Initial production version was Ki-61-IIa with armament as Ki-61-Ic; Ki-61-IIb as similar but with revised armament.

Ki-61-III: single prototype of proposed improved version.

Mitsubishi J2M *Raiden* 'Jack'

J2M1: initial prototypes; three built. Mitsubishi Kasei 13 engine.

J2M2: production aircraft; 151 built. Mitsubishi MK4R-A Kasei 23a engine.

J2M3: production aircraft; 260 built. Revised armament. The J2M3a featured further revised armament.

J2M3a: production aircraft; 21 built.

J2M4: prototypes; two built. Turbocharged engine.

J2M5: production aircraft; 34 built. Mitsubishi MK4U-4 engine. The J2M5a featured revised armament.

J2M6: production aircraft; one built. Revised cockpit, but otherwise similar to J2M3.

NB: While production of the J2M amounted to 476 by Mitsubishi, additional J2M5 aircraft were built by Koza Kaigun Kokusho.

Kawanishi N1K-J *Shiden* 'George'

N1K1-J: initial prototypes; nine built, 1942–43. Nakajima Homare 11 engine.

N1K1-J: production aircraft; 530 built by Kawanishi at Naruo, 1943–44, plus 468 built by Kawanishi at Himeji, 1943–45. Nakajima Homare 21 engine. N1K1-Ja and N1K1-Jb each

The white-bordered red lightning motif on this Ki-43-Ic indicates the aircraft was assigned to the 2nd Chutai, 50th Sentai. The fighter is also marked with an orange-yellow wing leading-edge identification panel.

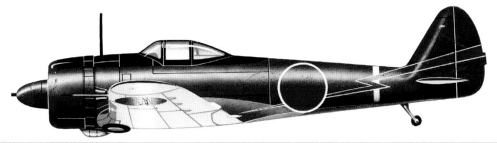

featured revised armament, while N1K1-Jc was a fighter-bomber variant.

N1K2-J: prototypes; eight built, 1943–44. Major redesign, with switch from mid-wing to low-wing configuration, lengthened fuselage, revised tail surfaces and revised undercarriage.

N1K2-J and N1K2-K: production aircraft; 351 built by Kawanishi at Naruo, 1944–45, plus 42 N1K2-J aircraft built by Kawanishi at Himeji, 1945. Additional production of the N1K2-J was undertaken by: Mitsubishi (nine, 1945), Aichi (one, 1945), Showa Hikoki (one, 1945), Dai-Juichi Kaigun Kokusho (one, 1945), and Omura Kaigun Kokusho (10, 1945). N1K2-J featured armament of N1K1-Jb, while N1K2-K was a two-seat trainer conversion.

N1K3-J: prototypes; two built, 1945. Engine moved forward to improve longitudinal stability. A proposed carrier-based N1K3-A version was not built.

N1K4-J: prototypes; two built, 1945. Nakajima Homare 23 engine. Armament as N1K3-J.

N1K4-A: prototype carrier-based fighter; one built, 1945.

N1K5-J: prototype; one almost completed but destroyed in USAAF air raid. Nakajima NK9H Homare 21 engine.

Nakajima Ki-84 *Hayate* 'Frank'

Ki-84: initial prototypes; two built, 1943.

Ki-84: service trials aircraft; 83 built, 1943–44.

Ki-84: pre-production aircraft; 42 built, 1944.

Ki-84-I and Ki-84-II: production aircraft; 3288 built, 1944–45, plus 94 Ki-84-I aircraft built by Mansyu Hikoki Seizo. Initial production aircraft was Ki-84-Ia, retaining armament of trials/pre-production aircraft; Ki-84-Ib and Ki-84-Ic each introduced revised armament. Ki-84-II introduced wood into the structure to conserve light alloys and was completed with either Ki-84-Ib or Ki-84-Ic armament.

Ki-113: prototype; one built by Nakajima, 1944. Primarily steel structure.

Ki-116: prototype; one built by Mansyu Hikoki Seizo, 1945. Lightweight powerplant, Mitsubishi Ha-33 engine. Converted from standard Ki-84-Ia.

Ki-106: prototypes; three built by Tachikawa, 1945. All-wood construction.

This two-view Ki-84-Ia was operated in the defence of the Japanese home islands in summer 1945. The aircraft was assigned to the 74th Sentai, which had previously flown Ki-43s and Ki-44s in the defence of Okinawa.

Kawasaki Ki-100

Ki-100: prototypes; three built, 1945. Converted from Ki-61-II airframes. Mitsubishi Ha-112-II engine.

Ki-100-Ia: production aircraft; 272 built, 1945. Converted from Ki-61-II airframes.

Ki-100-Ib: production aircraft; 106 built, 1945. Cut-down rear fuselage and bubble canopy, using airframe made for Ki-61-III.

Ki-100-II: prototypes; three built, 1945. Mitsubishi Ha-112-IIru turbocharged engine.

3: CARRIER AIRCRAFT

Aichi D1A 'Susie'

D1A1: prototypes and production aircraft; 162 built, 1934–37. Nakajima Kotobuki 2 Kai 1 engine.

D1A2: prototypes and production aircraft; 428 built, 1936–40. Nakajima Hikari 1 engine and other improvements including NACA engine cowling, wheel spats, improved windscreens.

Mitsubishi A5M 'Claude'

Ka-14: initial prototypes; six built, 1935–36.

A5M1, A5M2, A5M3 and A5M4: production aircraft; 782 built, 1936–40; plus 39 A5M4 aircraft built by K. K. Watanabe Tekkosho, 1939–42; and 161 A5M4 aircraft built by Dai-Nijuichi Kaigun Kokusho, 1939–41. Nakajima Kotobuki 2-Kai-3 engine in A5M1, generally similar A5M2a with Kotobuki 2-Kai-3 engine, and A5M2b with Kotobuki 3 engine. Two experimental A5M3 aircraft Hispano-Suiza 12xcrs engine. Major production version was A5M4.

A5M4-K: production aircraft, tandem two-seat trainer; 103 built by Dai-Nijuichi Kaigun Kokusho, 1942–44.

Ki-18: prototype; one built, 1935. Generally similar to Ka-14. Intended for Imperial Japanese Army.

Ki-33: prototypes; two built, 1936. Improved and re-engined Ki-33. Intended for Imperial Japanese Army.

Nakajima B5N 'Kate'

B5N1, B5N1-K and B5N2: prototypes and production aircraft; 669 built by Nakajima, 1936–41; plus 200 B5N2 aircraft built by Aichi, 1942–43; and 280 B5N2 aircraft built by Dai-Nijuichi Kaigun Kokusho, 1942–43. B5N1 was initial production version, superseded by improved B5N2 with more powerful engine. Some B5N1 aircraft also converted as B5N1-K trainers.

Aichi D3A 'Val'

11-Shi: initial prototypes; two built, 1937–38.

D3A1: service trials aircraft; six built, 1939.

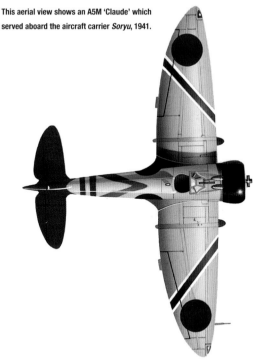

This aerial view shows an A5M 'Claude' which served aboard the aircraft carrier *Soryu*, 1941.

D3A1 Model 11: production aircraft; 470 built, 1939–42.

D3A2 Model 12: prototype; one built, 1942. Mitsubishi Kinsei 54 engine, increased fuel, modified rear canopy, propeller spinner.

D3A2 Model 22: production version of Model 12; 815 built by Aichi, 1942–44, plus 201 built by Showa Hikoki Kogyo, 1942–45.

Note also some D3A1 and D3A2 aircraft were later converted to become D3A2-K trainer versions.

Mitsubishi A6M *Reisen* 'Zeke'

(Production figures based on Japanese fiscal year reports, as cited in *Japanese Aircraft of the Pacific War*, R. J. Francillon)

A6M: all single-seat carrier-based and land-based fighter versions; 3879 built by Mitsubishi, 6570 built by Nakajima, for a grand total of 10,449 aircraft.

Annual breakdown of aircraft production as follows:

– 1939–42, 722 built by Mitsubishi, 115 by Nakajima;

– 1942–43, 729 built by Mitsubishi, 960 by Nakajima;

– 1943–44, 1164 built by Mitsubishi, 2268 by Nakajima;

– 1944–45, 1145 built by Mitsubishi, 2342 by Nakajima;

– April–August 1945, 119 built by Mitsubishi, 885 by Nakajima.

A6M2: The first two prototypes were A6M1 aircraft, with Zuisei 13 engine. The initial production version was the A6M2 Model 11 with Sakae 12 engine. From the 22nd aircraft, the A6M2 featured a reinforced rear spar. From the 65th aircraft, the A6M2 featured manual-folding wingtips, as the A6M2 Model 21.

A6M3: The improved A6M3 Model 32 had a Sakae 21 engine, and later aircraft had square-tipped wings. The A6M4 was an unsuccessful development with a turbocharged Sakae engine.

A6M5: The A6M5 Model 52 was an improved A6M3 with thicker wing skins, rounded wingtips and augmenting exhaust stacks. Sub-variants of the A6M5 included the A6M5a Model 52A with thicker skins and improved cannon; the A6M5b Model 52B with additional protection, fire-extinguishing system and revised armament; and the A6M5c Model 52C with additional pilot armour, revised armament, additional fuel capacity and unguided rocket capability.

A6M6: The A6M6c Model 53C was an improved A6M5c with Sakae 31 plus water/methanol boost and provision for centreline bomb and underwing drop tanks.

A6M7: The A6M7 Model 63 was a dive-bomber version of the A6M6c.

A6M8: The A6M8 Model 64 was a further improved version with Kinsei 62 engine, revised armament, improved protection.

A6M2-K: two-seat fighter trainer; 236 built by Dai-Nijuichi Kaigun Kokusho, 1943–45, plus 272 built by Hitachi Kokuki, 1944–45.

A6M5-K: two-seat fighter trainer; seven built by Hitachi Kokuki, 1945.

Yokosuka D4Y 'Judy'

13-Shi: initial prototypes; five built, 1940–41.

D4Y1: production aircraft; 660 built, 1942–44. Including D4Y1-C reconnaissance version and D4Y1 Kai with equipment for catapult launching.

D4Y2: improved production aircraft; 326 built, 1944. Aichi AE1P Atsuta 32 engine. Also D4Y2a with revised armament and D4Y2-C and D4Y2a-C reconnaissance versions and D4Y2 Kai with equipment for catapult launching. D4Y2-S was a night-fighter conversion of the D4Y2 with revised armament.

D4Y3: production aircraft; 536 built, 1944–45. Further improved version with Mitsubishi MK8P Kinsei engine. D4Y3a sub-variant was similar, but with armament of D4Y2a.

D4Y4: production aircraft; 296 built, 1945. Single-seat kamikaze aircraft based on D4Y3.

In addition to the above totals from Yokosuka production, a further 215 D4Y1, D4Y2 and D4Y3 production aircraft were built by Dai-Nijuichi Kaigun Kokusho.

Nakajima B6N *Tenzan* 'Jill'

14-Shi: initial prototypes; two built, 1941–42.

B6N1: production aircraft; 133 built, 1943. Nakajima MK7A Mamoru 11 engine.

B6N2: production aircraft; 1133 built, 1943–45. Introduced Mitsubishi Kasei engine. Also B6N2a with revised armament.

B6N3: prototypes; two land-based bombers built using B6N2 airframes. Mitsubishi MK4T-C Kasei 25C engine.

Aichi B7A *Ryusei* 'Grace'

B7A1: initial prototypes; nine built, 1942–44.

B7A2: production aircraft; 80 built by Aichi, 1944–45, plus 25 built by Dai-Nijuichi Kaigun Kokusho, 1944–45. One example of the B7A2 was completed with a Nakajima Homare 23 engine.

B7A3: Projected version with Mitsubishi MK9A engine.

This captured Zero was used by the Americans for test and evaluation purposes. The first Zero was captured in 1942, following the Japanese attack on Dutch Harbor in the Aleutian Islands.

4: FLYING BOATS AND FLOATPLANES

Mitsubishi F1M 'Pete'

F1M1: initial prototype; four built. Mitsubishi Zuisei 13 engine.

F1M2: production aircraft; 524 built by Mitsubishi; plus 590 built by Dai-Juichi Kaigun Kokusho.

Kawanishi H6K 'Mavis'

H6K1: initial prototypes; four built, 1936–38.

H6K1 Model 1: prototypes modified for production; three built, 1938. Mitsubishi Kinsei 43 engines.

H6K2 Model 11: production aircraft; 10 built, 1938–39. Similar to H6K1 but with minor equipment changes.

H6K2: modified as experimental transports; two built, 1939.

H6K3: modified as staff transports; two built, 1939. Based on H6K2 airframe.

H6K4 Model 22: production aircraft; 127 built, 1939–42. Major production version, increased fuel capacity, revised armament. Kinsei 46 engines introduced from August 1941.

H6K5 Model 23: production aircraft; 36 built, 1942. Final production version, revised armament, Kinsei 51 or 53 engines.

H6K2-L: transport version; 16 built, 1940–42. Civilian use with Japan Air Lines.

H6K4-L: transport version; 20 built, 1942–43. Kinsei 46 engines.

H6K4-L: transport version, modified from H6K4 airframes; two built, 1942.

Aichi E13A 'Jake'

E13A: prototypes and production aircraft; 113 built by Aichi, 1938–42; plus 48 production aircraft built by Dai-Juichi Kaigun Kokusho, 1940–42; and 1237 production aircraft built by Kyushu Hikoki, 1942–45. Major variants were E13A1a Model 11A with improved float bracing struts, propeller spinner and improved radio equipment, and E13A1b Model 11B with ASV radar provision.

Kawanishi H8K 'Emily'

H8K1: initial prototype; one built, 1940. Mitsubishi MK4A engines. Later converted to H8K1-L for transport duties, with Mitsubishi MK4Q engines.

H8K1: pre-production aircraft; two built, 1941.

H8K1: production aircraft; 14 built, 1941–42. Late production aircraft had Mitsubishi MK4B engines.

H8K2: production aircraft; 112 built, 1943–45. Major production version with MK4Q engines, increased armament, fully protected fuel tanks, ASV radar provision.

H8K3: prototypes; two built, 1944. Retractable wingtip floats and retractable dorsal turret.

H8K4: prototypes modified from H8K3 airframes; two built, 1945. Mitsubishi MK4T-B engines.

H8K2-L: transport version; 36 built, 1943–45. Developed from H8K1-L. Reduced armament.

Nakajima A6M2-N 'Rufe'

A6M2-N: prototypes and production aircraft; 327 built, 1941–43.

Aichi M6A *Seiran*

M6A1: prototypes; eight built, 1943–44.

M6A1: production aircraft; 18 built, 1944–45.

M6A1-K: prototypes; two built, 1945.

5: ROCKET AND JET-POWERED AIRCRAFT

Yokosuka MXY7 *Ohka*

Ohka Model 11: 155 built.

Ohka Model 22: 50 built. Slightly smaller version with reduced-size warhead and gas turbine engine.

Ohka Model K-1: 45 built. Training version.

Ohka Model 43 K-1 Kai: two built. Trainer version with retractable tailwheel landing gear, and without folding fin/rudder tip.

While the above totals detail production of the Ohka by Dai-Juichi Kaigun Koku Gijitsusho at Yokosuka, a further 600 examples were completed by Dai-Juichi Kaigun Kokusho at Kasumigaura.

Mitsubishi J8M *Shusui*

J8M: seven built, 1945.

MXY8: 'light' glider version, three built by Dai-Juichi Kaigun Kokusho.

Akigusa and Ku-13: 'heavy' glider version, 50–60 built by Maeda Koku Kenkyujo and Yokoi Koku.

Nakajima *Kikka*

Two aircraft built, 1945.

Allied Reporting Names for Japanese Aircraft

Allied reporting names were assigned to Japanese aircraft according to the following system:
• single- and twin-engined fighters: male first names
• reconnaissance seaplanes, bombers, attack bombers, dive-bombers, reconnaissance aircraft and
  flying boats: female first names
• trainers: names of trees
• gliders: names of birds

Allied reporting name	Manufacturer's designation	Japanese military designation	Remarks
'Abdul'	Nakajima Ki-27	Army Type 97 Fighter	Duplication for 'Nate'
'Adam'	Nakajima SKT-97	Navy Type 97 Fighter Seaplane	Fictional type
'Alf'	Kawanishi E7K	Navy Type 94 Reconnaissance Seaplane	
'Ann'	Mitsubishi Ki-30	Army Type 97 Light Bomber	
'Babs'		Mitsubishi Ki-15 and C5M	Army Type 97 Command Reconnaissance Aircraft/Navy Type 98 Reconnaissance Aircraft
'Baka'	Yokosuka MX7Y	Navy Special Attacker *Ohka*	
'Belle'	Kawanishi H3K1	Navy Type 90-2 Flying Boat	
'Ben'	Nagoya-Sento KI-001	Navy Carrier Fighter	Fictional type
'Bess'	Heinkel He 111		Erroneously believed to be in Japanese service
'Betty'	Mitsubishi G4M/G6M	Navy Type 1 Attack Bomber, Navy Type 1 Wingtip Convoy Fighter, Navy Type 1 Large Land Trainer, Navy Type 1 Transport	
'Bob'	Aichi ??	Navy Type 97 Reconnaissance Seaplane	Fictional type
'Bob'	Kawasaki Ki-28	Army Experimental Fighter	Erroneously believed to be in production
'Buzzard'	Kokusai Ku-7	Army Experimental Transport Glider Manazuru	
'Cedar'	Tachikawa Ki-17	Army Type 95-3 Primary Trainer	
'Cherry'	Yokosuka H5Y	Navy Type 99 Flying Boat	
'Clara'	Tachikawa Ki-70	Army Experimental Command Reconnaissance Aircraft	
'Claude'	Mitsubishi A5M	Navy Type 96 Carrier Fighter	

'Cypress'	Kyushu K9W and Kokusai Ki-86	Navy Type 2 Primary Trainer Momiji and Army Type 4 Primary Trainer	
'Dave'		Nakajima E8N	Navy Type 95 Reconnaissance Seaplane
'Dick'	Seversky A8V1	Navy Type S Two-seat Fighter	
'Dinah'	Mitsubishi Ki-46	Army Type 100 Command Reconnaissance Aircraft	
'Doc'	Messerschmitt Bf 110		Erroneously believed to be in IJA use
'Doris'	Mitsubishi B-97	Darai Medium Bomber	Fictional type
'Dot'	Yokosuka D4Y	Navy Carrier Bomber *Susei*	Duplication for 'Judy'
'Edna'	Mansyu Ki-71	Army Experimental Tactical Reconnaissance Aircraft	
'Emily'	Kawanishi H8K	Navy Type 2 Flying Boat	
'Eva' or 'Eve'	Mitsubishi Ohtori	Civil Long-Range Reconnaissance Aircraft	Erroneously believed to be bomber
'Frances'	Yokosuka P1Y	Navy Bomber Ginga, Navy Night Fighter Byakko, Navy Night Fighter *Kyokko*	
'Frank'	Mitsubishi TK-4	Army Type 0 Special Twin-engined Fighter	Fictional type; also 'Harry'
'Frank'	Nakajima Ki-84	Army Type 4 Fighter *Hayate*	Second use of name
'Fred'	Focke-Wulf Fw 190A		Erroneously believed to be in IJA use
'Gander'	Kokusai Ku-8	Army Type 4 Large Transport Glider	Previously 'Goose'
'George'	Kawanishi N1K-J	Navy Interceptor Fighter *Shiden*	
'Glen'	Yokosuka E14Y	Navy Type 0 Small Reconnaissance Seaplane	
'Goose'	Kokusai Ku-8	Army Type 4 Large Transport Glider	Later 'Gander'
'Grace'	Aichi B7A	Navy Carrier Attack Bomber *Ryusei*	
'Gus'	Nakajima AT-27	Twin-engined Fighter	Fictional type
'Gwen'	Mitsubishi Ki-21-IIb	Army Type 97 Heavy Bomber Model 2B	Later 'Sally III'
'Hamp'	Mitsubishi A6M3	Navy Type 0 Carrier Fighter Model 32	Initially 'Hap', then 'Hamp', finally 'Zeke 32'
'Hank'		Aichi E10A	Navy Type 96 Night Reconnais-sance Seaplane

'Harry'	Mitsubishi TK-4	Type 0 Special Twin-engined Fighter	Fictional type, previously 'Frank'
'Helen'	Nakajima Ki-49	Army Type 100 Heavy Bomber Donryu	
'Hickory'	Tachikawa Ki-54	Army Type 1 Advanced Trainer, Operational Trainer and Transport	
'Ida'	Tachikawa Ki-36 and Ki-55	Army Type 98 Direct Cooperation Aircraft and Type 99 Advanced Trainer	
'Ione'	Aichi AI-104	Navy Type 98 Reconnaissance Seaplane	Fictional type
'Irene'	Junkers Ju 87A		Erroneously believed to be in IJA use
'Irving'	Nakajima J1N	Navy Type 2 Reconnaissance Aircraft and Navy Night Fighter *Gekko*	
'Jack'	Mitsubishi J2M	Navy Interceptor Fighter *Raiden*	
'Jake'	Aichi E13A	Navy Type 0 Reconnaissance Seaplane	
'Jane'	Mitsubishi Ki-21	Army Type 97 Heavy Bomber	Later 'Sally'
'Janice'	Junkers Ju 88A	Erroneously believed to be in IJA use	
'Jean'	Yokosuka B4Y	Navy Type 96 Carrier Attack Bomber	
'Jerry'	Heinkel He 112B	Navy Type He Air Defence Fighter	
'Jill'	Nakajima B6N	Navy Carrier Attack Bomber *Tenzan*	
'Jim'	Nakajima Ki-43	Army Type 1 Fighter *Hayabusa*	Duplication of 'Oscar'
'Joe'	TK-19	Single-seat Fighter	Fictional type
'Joyce'	Tachikawa Ki-54	Type 1 Light Bomber	Misidentification of 'Hickory'
'Judy'	Yokosuka D4Y	Navy Type 2 Carrier Reconnaissance Aircraft and Navy Carrier Bomber *Susei*	
'Julia'		Type 97 Heavy Bomber	Misidentification of 'Lily'
'June'		Misidentification of 'Jake', believed to be floatplane version of 'Val'	
'Kate'	Mitsubishi B5M	Navy Type 97 Carrier Attack Bomber	Formerly 'Mabel'
'Kate'	Nakajima B5N	Navy Type 97 Carrier Attack Bomber	

'Laura'	Aichi E11A	Navy Type 98 Night Reconnaissance Seaplane	
'Lily'	Kawasaki Ki-48	Army Type 99 Twin-engined Light Bomber	
'Liz'	Nakajima G5N	Navy Experimental 13-Shi Attack Bomber Shinzan	
'Lorna'	Kyushu Q1W	Navy Patrol Aircraft *Tokai*	
'Louise'	Mitsubishi Ki-2	Army Type 93 Twin-engined Light Bomber	Also 'Loise'
'Luke'	Mitsubishi J4M	Navy Experimental 17-Shi Otsu Type Interceptor Fighter Senden	
'Mabel'	Mitsubishi B5M	Navy Type 97 Carrier Attack Bomber	Previously 'Kate'
'Mary'	Kawasaki Ki-32	Army Type 98 Light Bomber	
'Mavis'	Kawanishi H6K	Navy Type 97 Flying Boat	
'Mike'	Messerschmitt Bf 109E		Erroneously believed to be in IJA use
'Millie'	Vultee V-11GB	Type 98 Light Bomber	Erroneously believed to built in Japan
'Myrt'	Nakajima C6N	Navy Carrier Reconnaissance Aircraft Saiun	
'Nate'	Nakajima Ki-27	Army Type 97 Fighter	
'Nell'	Mitsubishi G3M/Yokosuka L3Y	Navy Type 96 Attack Bomber/ Navy Type 96 Transport	
'Nick'	Kawasaki Ki-45 Kai	Army Type 2 Two-seat Fighter *Toryu*	
'Norm'	Kawanishi E15K	Navy Type 2 High-speed Reconnaissance Seaplane Shiun	
'Norma'		Type 97 Light Bomber	Misidentified 'Babs'
'Oak'	Kyushu K10W	Navy Type 2 Intermediate Trainer	
'Omar'	Suzukaze 20	Twin-engined Fighter	Fictional type
'Oscar'	Nakajima Ki-43	Army Type 1 Fighter *Hayabusa*	Also known as 'Jim'
'Pat'	Tachikawa Ki-74		Initially identified as a fighter
'Patsy'	Tachikawa Ki-74	Army Experimental Long-range Bomber	
'Paul'	Aichi E16A	Navy Reconnaissance Seaplane	Zuiun
'Peggy'	Mitsubishi Ki-67	Army Type 4 Heavy Bomber *Hiryu*	
'Perry'	Kawasaki Ki-10	Army Type 95 Fighter	
'Pete'	Mitsubishi F1M	Navy Type 0 Observation Seaplane	

'Pine'	Mitsubishi K3M	Navy Type 90 Crew Trainer	
'Randy'	Kawasaki Ki-102b	Army Type 4 Assault Aircraft	
'Ray'		Mitsubishi Type 1 Fighter	Misidentified 'Zeke'
'Rex'	Kawanishi N1K	Navy Seaplane Fighter *Kyofu*	
'Rita'	Nakajima G8N	Navy Experimental 18-Shi Attack Bomber *Renzan*	
'Rob'	Kawasaki Ki-64	Army Experimental High-speed Fighter	
'Rufe'	Nakajima A6M2-N	Navy Type 2 Fighter Seaplane	
'Ruth'	Fiat BR.20	Army Type 1 Heavy Bomber	
'Sally'	Mitsubishi Ki-21	Army Type 97 Heavy Bomber	Formerly 'Jane'
'Sam'	Mitsubishi A7M	Navy Experimental 17-Shi Ko Type Carrier Fighter *Reppu*	
'Sandy'	Mitsubishi A5M	Navy Type 96 Carrier Fighter	Duplication of 'Claude'
'Slim'	Watanabe E9W	Navy Type 96 Reconnaissance Seaplane	
'Sonia'	Mitsubishi Ki-51	Army Type 99 Assault Aircraft	
'Spruce'	Tachikawa Ki-9	Army Type 95-1 Medium Trainer	
'Stella'	Kokusai Ki-76	Army Type 3 Command Liaison Aircraft	
'Steve'	Mitsubishi Ki-73	Army Experimental Fighter	
'Susie'	Aichi D1A	Navy Type 94 Carrier Bomber/ Navy Type 96 Carrier Bomber	
'Tabby'	Douglas L2D	Navy Type 0 Transport	
'Tess'	Douglas DC-2		
'Thalia'	Kawasaki Ki-56	Army Type 1 Freight Transport	
'Thelma'	Lockheed 14	Army Type LO Transport	
'Theresa'	Kokusai Ki-59	Army Type 1 Transport	
'Thora'	Nakajima Ki-34/L1N	Army Type 97 Transport/Navy Type 97 Transport	
'Tina'	Mitsubishi Ki-33	Army Type 96 Transport	Misidentified Yokosuka L3Y
'Tillie'	Yokosuka H7Y	Army Experimental 12-Shi Flying Boat	
'Toby'	Lockheed 14		
'Tojo'	Nakajima Ki-44	Army Type 2 Single-seat Fighter *Shoki*	
'Tony'	Kawasaki Ki-61	Army Type 3 Fighter *Hien*	
'Topsy'	Mitsubishi Ki-57/L4M	Army Type 100 Transport/Navy Type 0 Transport	

'Trixie'	Junkers Ju 52/3m		Erroneously believed to be in IJA use
'Trudy'	Focke-Wulf Fw 200		Erroneously believed to be in IJA use
'Val'	Aichi D3A Navy Type 99 Carrier Bomber		
'Willow'	Yokosuka K5Y	Navy Type 95 Intermediate Trainer	
'Zeke'	Mitsubishi A6M	Navy Type 0 Carrier Fighter	

Naming and Number Systems

Kitai numbers

In 1932 the IJA began to use Kitai numbers for aircraft, these being assigned in numerical order until 1944 (after which the numerals were assigned randomly, for additional secrecy). An aircraft, for example the Ki-61, retained its Kitai number throughout its development and service, and a unified system was applied to indicate successive production versions or modifications. As such, the Ki-61 designation indicated the basic project and prototype aircraft.

The Ki-61-Ia was the first production version of the first model (assigned the Roman numeral I). Ki-61-Ib was the second production version of the first model. The third production version of this aircraft represented a more significant modification and thus added a Kai (*Kaizo*) or modification suffix. Hence, the third production version was designated Ki-61-I Kai-c. The fourth production version was designated Ki-61-I Kai-d.

Once a second model was introduced, the prototypes were designated Ki-61-II (the Roman numeral II), and once modified these prototypes became the Ki-61-II Kai. The first production version of the second model was the Ki-61-II Kai-a, followed by the Ki-61-II Kai-b. A planned third model was assigned the designation Ki-61 III, and would have followed the same pattern had it yielded production aircraft.

Type numbers

In 1927 aircraft that were accepted for service received a designation that described their role and assigned a type number. The type number was based on the final two digits of the Japanese calendar year (e.g. year 2599 corresponded to 1939 in the Western calendar, and led to the type number 99). Further distinctions were made to identify successive models and versions, as in the Kitai system. For example, the Ki-61 in prototype form received

no type number. Once accepted for service as the Ki-61-Ia, a type number and description were assigned: Army Type 3 Fighter Model 1A, in which the numeral 3 corresponded with the Japanese year 2603. The Ki-61-Ia second production version of the first model became the Army Type 3 Fighter Model 1B.

While the Ki-61-II Kai prototypes again did not receive a type number, once the Ki-61-II Kai-a had been accepted for service, this first production version of the second model became the Army Type 3 Fighter Model 2A, followed by the Army Type 3 Fighter Model 2B (Ki-61-II Kai-b).

Imperial Japanese Navy aircraft nomenclature

The Imperial Japanese Navy utilized a different system to the Army. Beginning in 1931, a Shi number was assigned to each new experimental aircraft project, with the numeral relating to the Japanese calendar year and a description based on its intended role.

Once the aircraft had been accepted for IJN service, a short designation was introduced, e.g. A6M2. In this system, the first letter indicated the basic role of the aircraft (e.g. 'A' for carrier fighter, 'B' for carrier attack bomber – see full table on following pages). In this example, the first numeral indicated that this was the second such carrier fighter to have been ordered. The second letter, in this case 'M', revealed the identity of the manufacturer, namely Mitsubishi.

Each major modification of the basic aircraft led to a change in the second numeral; hence the A6M2 was the second major modification of the A6M. Adding a lower-case letter as a suffix, e.g. A6M5c, indicated a minor modification. If the aircraft was adapted to a role different from that originally envisaged, the designation would be altered in the format, e.g. A6M2-K.

An additional type number system was also used for aircraft entering production. This was based on a description of the aircraft's role and a type number relating to the Japanese calendar year (beginning in 1929, this was derived from the last two digits of that year). The only difference to the Army system of this type was that instead of Type 100 for 1940, the IJN expressed this as Type 0. The models and versions within this system were initially identified using Model 1 for the first iteration, and Model 1-1 for the first version thereof.

Beginning in the late 1930s, the designations for models and versions was revised, meaning that the first digit was changed when the airframe was modified and the second digit was changed when the engine was changed. In this way, the first model was designated Model 11, while Model 21 indicated an airframe modification, and Model 12 indicated a new engine in the existing airframe. If a new engine was introduced together with airframe modifications, the result was Model 22. A minor change (as in the A6M5c) would be reflected as Model 52C or, to give it its full designation, Navy Type 0 Carrier Fighter Model 52C.

After late 1942, in an effort to improve security, the type number system was altered such that the type number was removed and replaced with a name (the model number system remained unchanged). An example of this is the Aichi E16A1, which received the type number Navy Reconnaissance Seaplane Zuiun Model 11.

Japanese Navy Air Service Short Designation System

In the late 1920s a short designation scheme was introduced. This scheme used a letter to designate the type of aircraft, a numeral to indicate the number in a series of that type of aircraft, and a further letter to designate the manufacturer.

Letter	Type	Aircraft designation
A	Carrier Fighter	A1N1/A1N2
		A2N1/A2N3
		A3N1
		A4N1
		A5M1/A5M4
		A5M4-K
		A6M1/A6M8
		A6M2-K/A6M5-K
B	Carrier Attack Bomber (torpedo or level bomber)	B1M1/B1M3
		B2M1/B2M2
		B3Y1
		B4N1
		B4Y1
		B5M1
		B5N1/B5N2
		B6N1/B6N3
		B7A1/B7A3

C	Carrier Reconnaissance	C1M1/C1M2
		C2N1/C2N2
		C3N1
		C4A1
		C5M1/C5M2
		C6N1/C6N3
D	Carrier Bomber (dive bomber)	D1A1
		D1A2
		D2N1/D2N3
		D2Y1
		D3A1/D3A2
		D3M1
		D3N1
		D3Y1-K/D3Y2-K
		D4Y1/D4Y5
		D4Y1-C/D4Y2-Ca
		D5Y1
		DXD1
		DXHe1
E	Reconnaissance Seaplane	E1Y1/E1Y3
		E2N1/E2N2
		E3A1
		E4N1/E4N3
F	Observation Seaplane	F1A1
		F1K1
		F1M1/F1M2
G	Attack Bomber (land based)	G1M1
		G2H1
		G3M1/G3M3
		G4M1/G4M3
		G5N1/G5N2
		G6M1
		G6M1-K
		G6M1-L2
		G7M1
		G8N1/G8N3
		G9K1
		G10N1

H	Flying Boat (reconnaissance)	H1H1/H1H3
		H2H1
		H3H1
		H4H
		H5Y1
		H6K
		H8K
J	Land-based Fighter	J1N1
		J1N1-C/J1N1-R
		J1N1-S
		J2M1/J2M7
		J3K1
		J4M1
		J5N1
		J6K1
		J7W1/J7W2
		J8M1/J8M2
K	Trainer	K1Y1/K1Y2
		K2Y1/K2Y2
		K3M
		K5Y
		K7M
		K8W1
		K9W1
		K10W1
		K11W1
L	Transport	L1N1
		L2D1
		L2D2/L2D5
		L3Y1/L3Y2
		L4M1
		L7P1
M	Special Floatplane	M6A1
		M6A1-K
MX	Special Purpose Aircraft	MXJ1
		MXY1/MXY2
		MXY3

		MXY4
		MXY5
		MXY6
		MXY7
		MXY8
		MXY9
		MXY10
		MXY11
N	Seaplane Fighter	N1K1/N1K2
		N1K1-J
		N1K2-J/N1K5-J
		N1K2-K
P	Bomber (land based)	P1Y1/P1Y6
		P1Y1-S
		P1Y2-S
Q	Patrol Airplane (anti-submarine warfare)	Q1W1/Q1W2
		Q2M1
		Q3W1
R	Land-based Reconnaissance	R1Y1
		R2Y1/R2Y2
S	Night Fighter	S1A1

The aircraft carrier *Akagi* as she appeared in December 1941, with A6M fighters ranged on the deck aft.
Completed in March 1927, *Akagi* was the 'half-sister' to *Kaga,* and similarly served with the First Carrier
Division. For the attack on Pearl Harbor in December 1941, the *Akagi* carried 66 aircraft: 21 Mitsubishi
A6M Zeros, 18 Aichi D3A dive-bombers and 27 Nakajima B5N torpedo bombers.

Misubishi Ki-46 'Dinah'

CUTAWAY KEY

1 Starboard navigation light
2 Starboard wingtip
3 Wing front spar
4 Main spar
5 Auxiliary rear spar
6 Starboard aileron
7 Aileron hinges
8 Aileron actuating hinge fairing
9 Aileron fixed tab
10 Access plates
11 Control rods
12 Leading-edge fuel tank
13 Filler/access poirts
14 Rib station
15 Centre spar
16 Centre fuel tank
17 Aft fuel tank
18 Flap profile
19 Starboard flap outer section
20 Starboard nacelle aft fairing
21 Wing inner aft fuel tank
22 Wing inner centre fuel tank
23 Nacelle panels
24 Access
25 Engine bearer ring support
26 Cooling gills
27 Exhaust slots
28 Cowling inner ring
29 Inner trunking
30 Intake slot
31 Spinner
32 Three-blade propeller
33 Starter dog
34 Propeller hub
35 Reduction gear housing
36 Cowling nose ring
37 Mitsubishi Ha-112 Otsu radial engine
38 Exhaust manifold
39 Unstepped nose glazing
40 Inner coaming

41 Fixed frame
42 Nose panels
43 Nose landing lamp
44 Starboard mainwheel
45 Nose access/(optional) camera hatch
46 Nose (optional) fuel tank
47 Fuselage forward frame
48 Rudder pedal assembly
49 Control column
50 Throttle quadrant
51 Seat adjustment lever
52 Control horn
53 Compass housing
54 Starboard electrics panel
55 Canopy sliding section
56 Pilot's headrest
57 Pilot's 13-mm back armour
58 Pilot's seat and harness
59 Oxygen hose
60 Seat support frame
61 Control rod linkage
62 Wing root fillet
63 Wing front spar/fuselage frame
64 Main spar centresection carry-through
65 Wing control surface actuating rods
66 Canopy track
67 Canopy fixed aft glazing
68 Armoured headrest support
69 Aerial mast
70 Dorsal decking
71 Fuselage main (contoured cut-out fuel tank
72 Spring-loaded hand/entry grips
73 Cockpit former longeron
74 Fuel feed lines
75 Centre-section camera mounting rings
76 Ventral sliding hatch
77 Hatch actuating lever
78 Ventral glazing

79 Centre-section compartment
80 Centre-section camera stowage
81 Support frame
82 Fuselage structure
83 Dorsal identification light
84 Aerial
85 Aerial lead-in
86 Radio installation
87 Anti-vibration mountings
88 Centre-section side window
89 Main reconnaissance camera installation
90 Aft cockpit
91 Fixed glazing
92 Canopy sliding section
93 Canopy frames
94 Aft bulkhead
95 Canopy track
96 Dorsal gun stowage trough (deleted)
97 Canopy end glazing
98 Fuselage panelling
99 Fuselage structure
100 Fuselage frames
101 Tail surface control lines
102 Lifting tube
103 Tailfin root fairing
104 Starboard tailplane
105 Elevator balance
106 Starboard elevator
107 Elevator hinge
108 Tailfin leading edge
109 Tailfin forward spar
110 Tailfin structure
111 Aerial attachment
112 Rudder balance
113 Rudder upper hinge
114 Rudder frame
115 Rudder trim tab
116 Rudder actuating hinge
117 Rudder tab hinge fairing
118 Rudder post
119 Rudder contoured lower section
120 Tail navigation light
121 Elevator trim tab
122 Tab actuating hinge

123 Elevator frame
124 Elevator hinge
125 Elevator balance
126 Tailplane structure
127 Tailplane front spar
128 Control cables
129 Ribs
130 Tailplane tailfin front spar/fuselage integral member
131 Tailwheel retraction guide track
132 Shock absorber strut
133 Tailwheel retraction strut
134 Support frame
135 Retractable tailwheel
136 Tailwheel doors
137 Fuselage ventral panelling
138 Lower longeron
139 First-aid/access
140 Inspection/access panel
141 Fuselage skinning
142 Retractable crew entry step
143 Wing root fillet
144 Port flap inner structure
145 Port nacelle aft fairing
146 Port flap outer section
147 Flap profile
148 Aileron hinges
149 Aileron fixed tab
150 Port aileron frame
151 Aileron actuating hinge fairing
152 Port wingtip structure
153 Port navigation light
154 Front spar
155 Pitot tube
156 Wing ribs
157 Wing structure
158 Access panels
159 Wing main spar
160 Leading-edge fuel tank
161 Filler/access
162 Centre fuel tank
163 Aft fuel tank
164 Nacelle formers
165 Bulkhead frame

166 Engine bearer ring support attachment
167 Port nacelle oil tank
168 Exhaust slots
169 Wing inner centre fuel tank
170 Wing inner aft fuel tank
171 Wing main spar attachment
172 Wing front spar attachment
173 Leading-edge ribs
174 Cowling frame
175 Cowling inner frame
176 Engine bearer ring
177 Undercarriage retraction strut
178 Cooling gills
179 Mainwheel leg pivot
180 Engine bearer ring lower support strut
181 Exhaust
182 Mainwheel door
183 Mainwheel leg
184 Port mainwheel
185 Axle
186 Brake line
187 Torque links
188 Shock strut
189 Lower intake
190 Engine cowling nose ring
191 Inner ring
192 Gear housing
193 Three-blade Sumitomo propeller
194 Spinner
195 Starter dog
196 Propeller hub
197 Intake trunking
198 Intake slot
199 Ventral (centreline) tank pylon
200 Auxiliary ventral fuel tank (101 Imp gal/460 litre capacity) Mitsubishi Ki-46-III

SPECIFICATION Ki-46-III Kai

Type

Two-seat reconnaissance aircraft

Powerplant

Two 1119kW (1500hp) Mitsubishi Ha-112-II radial piston engines

Performance

Maximum speed: 630 km/h (391mph) at 6000m (19,685ft); service ceiling: 10500m (34,450ft); range: 4000km (2485 miles); weight (empty) 3830kg (8444lb); maximum take-off 6500kg (14,330lb)

Dimensions

Wingspan: 14.70m (48ft 2.75in); length: 11.00m (36 ft 1in); height: 12 ft 8.75in (3.88m); wing area: 32.00 m² (344.46sqft)

Armament

Ki-46-I and Ki-46-II had a single 7.7mm (0.303in) rear-firing machine-gun on a trainable mount; III Kai two 20mm Ho-5 and oblique 37 Ho-203

This cutaway shows the Mitsubishi Ki-46-III. This improved model first flew in December 1942. It had a significantly higher speed (630km/h/391mph) than the early version, with more powerful, fuel-injected Mitsubishi Ha-112 engines.

Kawasaki Ki-61 *Hien* 'Tony'

CUTAWAY KEY

1 Starboard navigation light
2 Wing rib bracing
3 Wing spar
4 Starboard aileron
5 Aileron tab
6 Starboard flap
7 Wing gun access panel
8 Gun port
9 Three-blade constant-speed propeller
10 Auxiliary drop-tank (43.9 Imp gal/200 litres)
11 Propeller boss
12 Propeller reduction gear housing
13 Air intake duct
14 Starboard mainwheel
15 Lower cowling quick-release catches
16 Exhaust stubs
17 Anti-vibration mounting pad
18 Engine bearer
19 Upper cowling quick-release catches
20 Kawasaki Ha-40 (Army Type 2) engine
21 Engine accessories
22 Gun port
23 Cannon barrels
24 Firewall
25 Cowling panel line
26 Supercharger
27 Supercharger intake
28 Ammunition tanks
29 Ammunition feed chute
30 Two 20mm Ho-5 cannon
31 Sloping windscreen
32 Gunsight
33 Control column
34 Pilot's seat (armoured)
35 Fuselage frame
36 Rearward-sliding cockpit
37 Pilot's headrest
38 Rear-vision cut-out
39 Aft glazing
40 Canopy track
41 Spring-loaded handhold
42 Fuselage fuel tank (36.2 Imp gal/165 litres)
43 Fuselage equipment access door (upward hinged)
44 Radio pack (Type 99-111)
45 Aerial mast
46 Aerial lead-in
47 Aerial
48 Elevator control cables
49 Upper longeron
50 Rudder cable
51 Fuselage join
52 Starboard tailplane
53 Starboard elevator
54 Tailfin root fairing
55 Tailfin structure
56 Rear navigation light (port and starboard)
57 Aerial stub mast
58 Rudder balance
59 Rudder fixed trim tab
60 Rudder post
61 Rudder framework
62 Elevator tab
63 Elevator fixed trim tab
64 Port elevator
65 Elevator control cable
66 Rudder hinge
67 Rear fuselage frame/tailplane attachment
68 Tailwheel retraction jack
69 Tailwheel doors
70 Retractable tailwheel
71 Tailwheel shock absorber oleo
72 Lower longeron
73 Radiation bath air outlet
74 Adjustable gill
75 Radiator
76 Radiator intake ducting
77 Intake
78 Main spar/fuselage attachment point
79 Inboard mainwheel doors
80 Mainwheel well
81 Landing light
82 Mainwheel pivot point
83 Mainwheel leg
84 Oleo shock-absorber section (leather-sleeved)
85 Mainwheel single fork
86 Port mainwheel
87 Mainwheel door
88 Separate mainwheel leg fairing
89 Gun port
90 Machine gun barrel
91 Wing-mounted 12.7mm Ho-103 machine-gun
92 Gun access panel
93 Bomb/tank shackle
94 Port flap
95 Main spar
96 Wing ribs
97 Auxiliary drop-tank (43.9 Imp gal/200 litres)
98 Pitot head
99 Metal wing skin
100 Aileron tab
101 Port aileron
102 Wingtip structure
103 Port navigation light

Ki-61-KAIs of the Akeno Flying Training School, the main home-based Hien training unit, are run up before another training sortie. KAI variants had strengthened wings and cannon armament.

SPECIFICATION Ki-61-I-Otsu

Type

Single-seat fighter

Powerplant

One 876kW (1175hp) Kawasaki Ha-40 V-12 piston engine

Performance:

Maximum speed: 560km/h (348mph); service ceiling: 10000m (32,810ft); maximum range: 1900km (1181 miles)

Weights

Empty: 2630kg (5798lb); maximum take-off: 3470kg (7650lb)

Dimensions

Wingspan: 12.00m (39ft 4.5in); length: 8.95m (29ft 4.25in); height: 3.70m (12ft 11in); wing area: 20.00m² (215.29sqft)

Armament

Two 12.7mm (.50in) Ho-103 machine guns; two 20mm (0.78in) Ho-5 cannon

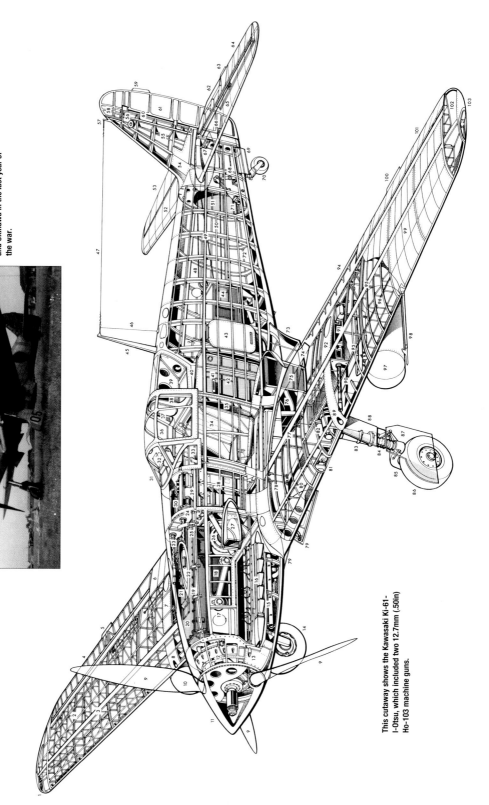

This Ki-61-I of the 37th Sentai was among those that fought in the last stages of the defence of the Philippines, before being forced to redeploy to Formosa and Okinawa in the last year of the war.

This cutaway shows the Kawasaki Ki-61-I-Otsu, which included two 12.7mm (.50in) Ho-103 machine guns.

Mitsubishi A6M2 Reisen 'Zeke'

CUTAWAY KEY

1 Tail navigation light
2 Tail cone
3 Tailfin fixed section
4 Rudder lower brace
5 Rudder tab (ground adjustable)
6 Fabric-covered rudder
7 Rudder hinge
8 Rudder post
9 Rudder upper hinge
10 Rudder control horn (welded to torque tube)
11 Aerial attachment
12 Tailfin leading edge
13 Forward spar
14 Tailfin structure
15 Tailfin nose ribs
16 Port elevator
17 Port tailplane
18 Piano-hinge join
19 Fuselage dorsal skinning
20 Control turnbuckles
21 Arrester hook release/retract steel cable runs
22 Fuselage frame/ tailplane centre brace
23 Tailplane attachments
24 Elevator cables
25 Elevator control horns/torque tube
26 Rudder control horns
27 Tailwheel combined retraction/shock strut
28 Elevator trim tab
29 Tailwheel leg fairing
30 Castored tailwheel
31 Elevator frame (fabric-covered)
32 Elevator outer hinge
33 Tailplane structure
34 Forward spar
35 Elevator trim tab control rod (chaindriven)
36 Fuselage flotation bag rear wall
37 Arrester hook (exterded)
38 Arrester hook pivot mounting
39 Elevator trim tab cable guide
40 Fuselage skinning
41 Fuselage frame stations
42 Arrester hook position indicator cable (duralumin tube)
43 Elevator cables
44 Rudder cables
45 Trim tab cable runs
46 Arrester hook pulley guide
47 Fuselage stringers
48 Fuselage flotation bag front
49 Fuselage construction join
50 Wingroot fillet formers
51 Compressed air cylinder (wing gun charging)
52 Transformer
53 'Ku' type radio receiver
54 Oxygen cylinder (starboard)
carbon dioxide fire extinguisher cylinder (port)
55 Battery
56 Radio tray support
57 Radio transmitter
58 Canopy/fuselage fairing
59 Aerial mast support/lead-in
60 Aerial
61 Aerial mast (forward raked)
62 Canopy aft fixed section
63 Aluminium and plywood canopy frame
64 Crash bulkhead/ headrest support
65 'Ku' type D/F frame antenna mounting (late models)
66 Canopy track
67 Turnover truss
68 Pilot's seat support frame
69 Starboard elevator control bell crank
70 Aileron control push-pull rod
71 Wing rear spar/ fuselage attachment
72 Fuselage aft main double frame
73 Aileron linkage
74 Landing-gear selector lever
75 Flap selector lever
76 Seat adjustment lever
77 Pilot's seat
78 Cockpit canopy rail
79 Seat support rail
80 Elevator tab trim handwheel
81 Fuel gauge controls
82 Throttle quadrant
83 Reflector gunsight mounting (offset to starboard)
84 Sliding canopy
85 Plexiglas panels
86 Canopy lock/release
87 Windscreen
88 Fuselage starboard 0.303in (7.7mm) machine-gun
89 Control column
90 Radio control box
91 Radio tuner
92 Elevator control linkage
93 Rudder pedal bar assembly
94 Cockpit underfloor fuel
95 Wing front spar/ fuselage attachment
96 Fuselage forward main double frame
97 Ammunition magazine
98 Ammunition feed
99 Blast tube
100 Cooling louvres
101 Fuselage fuel tank capacity 34 Imp gal (155 litres)
102 Firewall bulkhead
103 Engine bearer lower attachment
104 Engine bearer upper attachment
105 Oil tank capacity 12.7 Imp gal (58 litres)
106 Bearer support struts
107 Cooling gill adjustment control
108 Machine-gun muzzle trough
109 Barrel fairing
110 Oil filler cap
111 Fuselage fuel tank filler cap
112 Port flap profile
113 Port fuselage machine-gun
114 Port wing gun access panels
115 Port inner wing identification light
116 Port wing flotation bag inner wall
117 Wing spar joins
118 Aileron control rods
119 Port aileron (fabric covered)
120 Aileron tab (ground adjustable)
121 Aileron external counter-balance
122 Control linkage
123 Wing skinning
124 Port inner wing identification light
125 Port navigation light lead conduit
126 Wingtip hinge
127 Wing end rib
128 Port wing flotation bag outer wall
129 Wingtip structure
130 Port wingtip (folded)
131 Port navigation light
132 Port wingtip hinge release catch
134 Wing leading-edge skinning
135 Wing front spar
136 Port wing gun muzzle
137 Port undercarriage visual indicator
138 Undercarriage hydraulics access
139 Nacelle gun troughs
140 Cooling gills
141 Fuselage gun synchronization cable
142 Bearer support strut assembly
143 Carburettor
144 Exhaust manifold
145 Cowling panel fastener clips
146 950 hp Nakajima Sakae 12 radial engine
147 Cowling inner ring profile
148 Cowling nose ring
149 Three-bladed propeller
150 Spinner
151 Propeller gears
152 Hub
153 Carburettor intake
154 Port main wheel
155 Oil cooler intake
156 Exhaust outlet
157 Starboard mainwheel inner door fairing
158 Engine bearer support brace
159 Oil cooler
160 Wingroot fasteners
161 Starboard mainwheel well
162 Front auxiliary spar cutouts
163 Auxiliary fuel tank
165 Intake trunking
166 Front main spar
167 Starboard wing fuel tank capacity 43 Imp gal (195 litres)
168 Fuel filler cap
169 Rear main spar
170 Flap actuating cylinder
171 Access cover
172 Starboard flap structure
173 Starboard inner wing identification light
174 Starboard wing 20-mm cannon
175 Access panels
176 Ammunition magazine (underwing loading)
177 Landing gear hydraulic retraction jack
178 Hydraulic lines
179 Starboard undercarriage visual indicator
180 Landing gear pivot axis
181 Undercarriage/spar mounting
182 Starboard wing gun muzzle
183 Starboard undercarriage leg
184 Oleo travel
185 Welded steel wheel fork
186 Wheel uplock latch
187 Starboard mainwheel
188 Wheel door fairing ball and swivel closure
189 Mainwheel door fairing
190 Axle hub
191 Access plate
192 Hinge
193 Left fairing attachments
194 Brake line
195 Leg fairing
196 Leg fairing upperflap
197 Wing gun barrel support collar
198 Wing nose ribs
199 Cartridge ejection chute
200 Oil cooler intake
201 Wing outer structure
202 Front spar outer section
203 Inter-spar ribs
204 Rear spar outer section
205 Aileron control access
206 Aileron (ground adjustable)
207 Starboard aileron frame
208 Aileron external counter balance
209 Control linkage
210 Starboard wingtip (folded)
211 Starboard outerwing identification light
212 Aileron outer hinge
213 Starboard wing flotation bag
214 Wing end rib
215 Starboard wingtip hinge release catch
216 Wingtip structure
217 Starboard navigation light

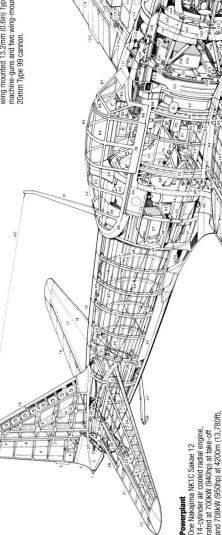

SPECIFICATION A6M2
Model 21

Dimensions
Wingspan: 12m (39ft 4.55in)
A6M3, 5, 8: 11m (36ft 11.1in)
Length (including A6M3): 12m (39ft 4.5in)
A6M5: 9.12m (29ft 11.1in)
A6M8: 9.24m (30ft 32in)
Height: 3.05m (10ft)
A6M3, 5: 3.51m (11ft 6.16in)
Wing area: 22.44m² (241.541sqft)
A6M3: 21.53m² (231.746sqft)
A6M5, 8: 21.30m² (229.27sqft)

Powerplant
One Nakajima NK1C Sakae 12
14-cylinder air cooled radial engine,
rated at 700kW (940hp) at take-off
and 708kW (950hp) at 4200m (13,780ft),
driving a three-bladed metal propeller.
A6M3, 5a, b, c: One Nakajima NK1F
Sakae 21 14-cylinder air cooled radial
engine, rated at 843kW (1130hp) at
take-off and 820kW (1100hp) at
2850m (9,350ft) and 731kW (980hp)
at 6000m (19,685ft), driving a
threebladed metal propeller.

Weights
Empty: 1680kg (3704lb)
A6M3: 1807kg (3984lb)
A6M5: 1876kg (4136lb)
A6M8: 2150kg (4740lb)
Loaded: 2410kg (5313lb)
A6M3: 2544kg (5609lb)
A6M5: 2733kg (6025lb)
A6M8: 3150kg (6945lb)
Maximum: 2796kg (6164lb)
Wing loading: 107.4kg/m² (22lb/sq ft)
A6M3: 118.1kg/m² (24.2lb/sq ft)
A6M5: 128.3kg/m² (26.3lb/sq ft)
A6M8: 147.9kg/m² (30.3lb/sq ft)

Fuel and load
Normal fuel: 590.98 litres (130 Imp gal)
A6M3: 609.16 litres (134 Imp gal)
Maximum fuel: 918.29 litres (202 Imp gal)
External fuel: 330 litres (72.6 Imp gal)
Maximum weapon load: 811.92kg
(1,790lb)

Performance
Maximum speed: 288kt (332mph;
534km/h) at 4550m (14,930ft)
A6M3: 294kt (338mph; 545km/h) at
6000m (19,685ft)
A6M5: 305kt (351mph; 565km/h) at
19.685ft (6000m)
A6M8: 309kt (365mph; 573km/h) at
19.685ft (6000m)

Cruising speed: 180kt (207mph;
334km/h)
A6M3, 5: 200kt (230mph; 370km/h)
Service ceiling: 32,810ft (10,000m)
A6M3: 36,250ft (11,050m)
A6M5: 38,520ft (11,740m)
A6M8: 37,075ft (11,200m)

Range
Normal range: 1010nm (1160
miles/1867km)
Maximum range: 1675nm (1930 miles/
1162km)

Armament
Fixed: Two 7.7mm (0.303in) Type 97
machine-guns in the upper fuselage
decking and two wing-mounted 20mm
Type 99 cannon. The A6M8 carried two
wing mounted 13.2mm (0.6in) Type 3
machine-guns and two wing-mounted
20mm Type 99 cannon.

External: Normal load was two 60kg
(132lb) bombs. For suicide missions,
one 250kg (551lb) bomb was carried.
Maximum external load for A6M7 and
A6M8 was 500kg (1102lb). Eight 10kg
(22lb) or two 60kg (132lb) air-to-air
rockets could be carried by the A6M6c
and A6M8.
There were also hardpoints for drop
tanks; usually a 330 litre (72.6 Imp
gal) tank was carried, but the A6M7
and A6M8 carried a 350 litre (77 Imp
gal) tank.

This cutaway shows the Mitsubishi Zero
A6M2 Model 21. The Model 21 included
folding wingtips, making it suitable for
aircraft carrier operations, and became
one of the most produced versions of the
early war.

Mitsubishi G4M 'Betty'

CUTAWAY KEY

1 Starboard navigation light
2 Starboard wingtip
3 Wing outboard spars
4 Starboard aileron
5 Aileron hinges
6 Aileron tab linkage
7 Fixed tab
8 Aileron trim tab
9 Wing join station
10 Flap hinge fairings
11 Starboard flap
12 Flap controls
13 Wing spar
14 Starboard wing fuel tanks
15 Starboard outer oil tank
16 Engine nacelle fairing
17 Cooling gills
18 Individual exhaust stubs
19 Engine bearer
20 Intake
21 Cowling ring
22 Four-blade propeller
23 Spinner
24 7.7mm Type 92 machine-gun
25 Nose turret
26 Nose radar antenna
27 Nose turret drive mechanism
28 Bomb-aimer's flat panel
29 Bomb-aimer's couch
30 Type 90 bombsight
31 Additional cheek gun/drift sight mounting (port and starboard)
32 Bomb panel
33 Ammunition magazine stowage
34 Nose glazing
35 Additional machine-gun (stowed)
36 Rudder pedal assembly
37 Control console
38 Coaming
39 Flat windscreen panels
40 Overhead controls
41 Sun blinds
42 Flight deck emergency escape hatch
43 Pilot's seats
44 Control column
45 Rudder pedal assembly
46 Bomb-aimer's seat
47 Control linkage
48 Flight deck floor level
49 Nose compartment access walkway
50 Fuselage structure
51 Navigation/wireless-operator's station
52 Equipment racks
53 Commander's seat
54 Cockpit roof glazing
55 Front spar carry-through
56 Fuselage centre-section fuel tanks
57 Front spar/fuselage attachment
58 Over-spar centre step section
59 Rear spar carry-through
60 Rear spar/fuselage attachment
61 Gunner's take-off/land jump seats
62 Emergency handhold (down to wing upper surface)
63 Emergency escape hatch
64 Dorsal frames
65 Intake scoop
66 Fuselage window
67 Dorsal gunner's step
68 Dorsal turret mount
69 Ammunition magazine stowage
70 Strengthened longeron section
71 Turret drive mechanism
72 Dorsal turret
73 20mm Type 99 dorsal cannon
74 Aerial mast
75 Fuselage structure
76 Oxygen cylinders
77 Stepped fuselage floor
78 Gunner's seat
79 Fuselage window
80 Waist gun position
81 Ammunition magazine stowage
82 Gun mounting
83 20mm Type 99 cannon
84 Fixed upper glazing
85 Sliding (upwards) window section
86 Starboard (asymmetric) waist gun position
87 Fuselage frames
88 Longerons
89 Cannon muzzle trough
90 Crew circular entry hatch
91 Latch
92 Walkway to tail turret
93 Fuselage window
94 Starboard radar aerial internal support
95 Aft fuselage structure
96 Fuselage frame/tailfin support
97 Tailfin join
98 Starboard tailplane skinning
99 Elevator balance
100 Aerial
101 Starboard elevator
102 Elevator tab
103 Tailfin leading edge
104 Tailfin structure
105 Aerial attachment
106 Rudder balance
107 Rudder frame
108 Rudder post
109 Access panels
110 Rudder tab
111 Rudder tab linkage
112 Rudder lower hinge
113 Fixed lower section fillet
114 Tail navigation light
115 Aft fuselage glazing
116 Open tail turret (glazed side segments)
117 Tail 20mm Type 99 cannon
118 Elevator tab
119 Port elevator
120 Elevator balance
121 Tailplane structure
122 Tail gunner's seat

SPECIFICATION G4M2 Model 22 Otsu

Type

Seven-crew long-range bomber

Powerplant

Two 1342kW (1800hp) Mitsubishi MK4T Kasei 25 radial piston engines

Performance

Maximum speed: 438km/h (272mph) at 4600m (15,090ft); service ceiling: 8950m (29,365ft); maximum range: 6059km (3765 miles)

Weights

Empty: 18,049lb (8350kg); maximum take-off: 27,558lb (12500kg)

Dimensions

Wingspan: 25m (82ft 0.25in); length: 20m (65ft 7.5in); height: 6.00m (19ft 8.25in); wing area: 78.13m² (841.01sqft)

123 Tailplane/fuselage frame attachment
124 Tail gun ammunition magazine feed
125 Tail surface control linkage
126 Walkway
127 Port radar antenna
128 Support strut
129 Tailwheel shock strut
130 Non-retractable tailwheel
131 Lower longeron
132 Waist station floor level
133 Bulged bomb-bay aft contour
134 Port flap section
135 Wing structure
136 Rear main spar
137 Wing inboard/outboard join
138 Aileron trim tab
139 Fixed tab
140 Port aileron
141 Wing ribs
142 Port wingtip
143 Port navigation light
144 Front main spar
145 Panel joins
146 Nose ribs
147 Port wing fuel tanks (four)
148 Spar join
149 Port wing oil tanks (two)
150 Undercarriage attachment
151 Nacelle fairing
152 Mainwheel leg
153 Oleo cuff
154 Brake line
155 Port mainwheel
156 Mainwheel doors
157 Engine lower intake
158 Cooling gills
159 Individual exhaust stubs
160 Cooling/exhaust stubs
161 Mainwheel bay
162 Mitsubishi Kasei 25 (MK4T) engine
163 Engine upper intake
164 Four-blade Sumitomo VDM propeller
165 Propeller hub
166 Spinner
167 Bulged bomb-bay forward contour
168 Pitot tube (offset/angled to starboard)
169 D/F loop
170 Weapons load, inc:
171 Twelve 110lb (50kg) bombs (4 x 3)
172 Four 551lb (250kg) bombs (2 x 2)
173 Two 1102lb (500kg) bombs
174 One naval torpedo, or
175 One 1764lb (800kg) bomb

This cutaway shows the Mitsubishi G4M2 Model 22 Otsu, which included the longer-barreled 20 mm (0.787 in) Type 99 Model 2 cannon in the dorsal turret.

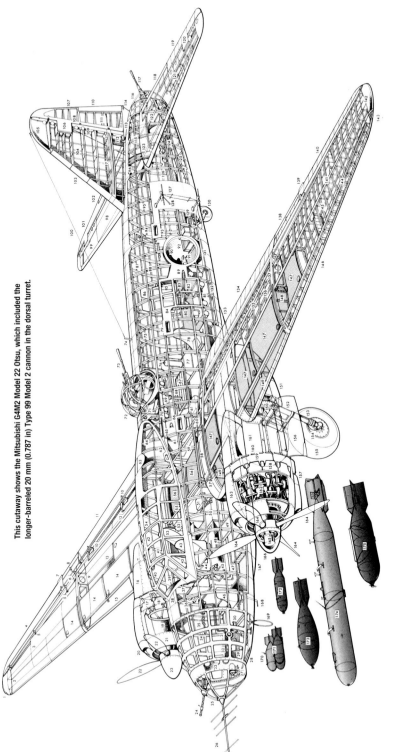

The 'Flying Cigar' appellation is fully justified in this view of a G4M1. Built in larger numbers than any other Japanese bomber, the type saw considerable success in long-range bombing duties.

Nakajima Ki-43 *Hayabusa* 'Oscar'

CUTAWAY KEY

1 Starboard navigation light
2 Wingtip
3 Starboard fabric-covered aileron
4 Aileron actuating linkage
5 Aileron control rod
6 Control rod connecting fittings
7 Aileron tab
8 Flap outer cable drum
9 Flap travel
10 Flap control cables
11 Radio mast
12 Light alloy wing skinning
13 Starboard undercarriage fairing
14 Gun port fairings
15 Nose ring
16 Annular oil cooler
17 Two-blade two-pitch metal propeller
18 Spinner
19 Starter dog
20 Supercharger air intake
21 Intake fairing
22 Nakajima Ha-25 (Type 99) 14-cylinder two-row radial engine
23 Cowling gills
24 Exhaust collector ring
25 Exhaust outlet
26 Engine lower bearers
27 Oil regulator valve
28 Oil pressure tank
29 Engine accessories
30 Engine upper bearers
31 Cowling gill controls
32 Two 12.7mm (0.5in) Type 89 machine-guns
33 Gun gas outlet
34 Cartridge link ejection chute
35 Fireproof (No. 1) bulkhead
36 Ammunition magazine (500 rpg)
37 Cartridge ejection chute
38 Gun breech fairing
39 Telescopic gun sight
40 One-piece curved windscreen
41 Radio aerial
42 Aft-sliding cockpit canopy
43 Turnover structure
44 Seat back
45 Seat adjustment rails
46 Seat pan
47 Throttle quadrant
48 Instrument panel
49 Control column
50 Rudder pedals
51 Underfloor control linkage
52 Seat support frame
53 Control cable and rod bearings
54 Oxygen cylinders
55 Rudder cable pulleys
56 Transceiver
57 Type 96 Hi-3 radio installation
58 Receiver unit
59 Transmitter unit
60 Anti-vibration mounting slings
61 Fuselage construction break
62 Inspection/access panel
63 Fuselage stringers
64 Fuselage structure

65 Frame
66 Fuselage upper longeron
67 Elevator control cables
68 Fuselage skinning
69 Tailwheel shock strut
70 Tail unit attachment
71 Tailfin root fairing
72 Starboard tailplane
73 Elevator balance
74 Starboard elevator
75 Tailfin leading edge
76 Tailfin structure
77 Rear navigation light
78 Aerial attachment
79 Rudder upper hinge
80 Rudder post
81 Rudder frame
82 Rudder trim tab
83 Rudder middle hinge
84 Elevator control lever
85 Elevator trim tab
86 Elevator frame
87 Elevator balance
88 Tailplane structure
89 Rudder control lever
90 Non-retractable tailwheel
91 Cantilever tailwheel leg
92 Tailwheel leg/bulkhead attachment
93 Rudder cables
94 Fuselage skinning
95 Wing fillet
96 Flap inboard profiles
97 Flap actuating cylinder
98 Rear spar/fuselage

99 Main spar/fuselage attachment
100 Front spar/fuselage attachment
101 Port main fuel tank (29.5 Imp gal/132 litre capacity)
102 Port overload fuel tank (33 Imp gal/150 litre capacity)
103 Fuel filler caps
104 Main spar
105 Rear spar
106 Aileron control rod
107 Flap inboard travel
108 Flap pulley fairing
109 Fowler-type 'butterfly' combat flap
110 Flap outboard travel
111 Aileron trim tab
112 Aileron inner hinge
113 Aileron centre hinge/control rod attachment
114 Port aileron
115 Aileron outer hinge
116 Port wingtip
117 Port navigation light
118 Wing skinning
119 Pitot head
120 Leading edge ribs
121 Front spar
122 Landing light
123 Mainwheel leg fairing
124 Torque links
125 Port mainwheel
126 Axle fork
127 Mainwheel oleo
128 Mainwheel leg pivot
129 Gear support bearer
130 Gear actuating cylinder

131 Emergency actuation cables
132 Leading edge rib cut-outs
133 Mainwheel well
134 Underwing drop tank pylon (mounted aft and just inboard of the main undercarriage attachment point)
135 Tank suspension lugs
136 Air vent
137 Fuel pipe connection
138 Tank fin
139 Sway brace attachment points
140 Jettisonable 200-litre (44 Imp gal) tank

SPECIFICATION Ki-43-IIb

Type

Single-seat fighter/fighter-bomber

Powerplant

One 858kW (1150hp) Nakajima Ha-115 radial piston engine

Performance

Maximum speed: 530km/h (329mph) at 4000m (13,125ft);
service ceiling: 11,200m (36,745ft); maximum range: 3200km
(1988 miles)

Weights

Empty: 1910kg (4211lb); maximum take-off: 2590kg (5710lb)

Dimensions

Wingspan: 10.84m (35ft 6.75in); length: 8.92m (29ft 3.25in);
height: 3.27m (10ft 8.75in); wing area: 21.40m² (230.36sqft)

Armament

Two 12.7mm (0.50in) forward firing machine-guns, plus two
underwing racks each able to carry a 250kg (551lb) bomb

This cutaway shows the Nakajima
Ki-43-IIb Otsu, which included an
armoured back of the pilot seat and
additional drop tanks on later models.

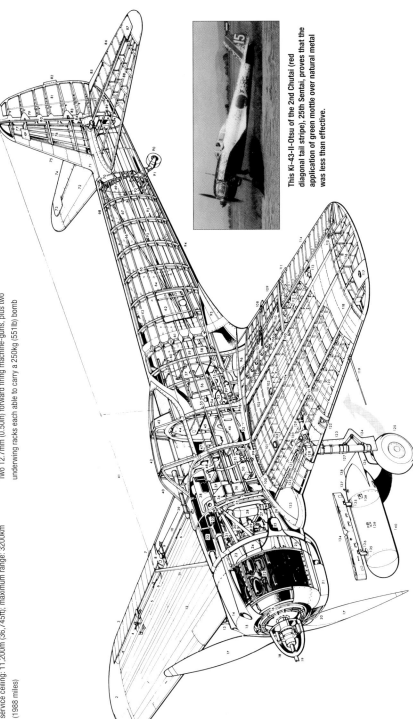

This Ki-43-II-Otsu of the 2nd Chutai (red
diagonal tail stripe), 25th Sentai, proves that the
application of green mottle over natural metal
was less than effective.

Nakajima Ki-84 *Hayate* 'Frank'

CUTAWAY KEY

1 Starter dog
2 Spinner
3 Constant-speed electrically operated Pe-32 propeller
4 Propeller reduction gear housing
5 Carburettor air intake
6 Starboard 20-mm Ho-5 cannon muzzle
7 Gun camera port
8 Starboard leading-edge fuel tank (67 litre/14.7 Imp gal capacity)
9 Mainspar
10 Starboard navigation light
11 Starboard wingtip
12 Fabric-covered aileron
13 Aileron control link fairing
14 Aileron trim tab
15 Flap track extension fairing
16 Starboard Fowler-type flap
17 Wing cannon ammunition box access
18 Wing cannon access covers
19 Carburettor intake trunking
20 Machine-gun blast tube
21 (Nakajima Ha-45–21) 18-cylinder radial air-cooled engine
22 Army Type 4 Model
23 Cowling fasteners
24 Aluminium cylinder' fans
25 Oil cooler intake
26 Starboard mainwheel
27 Oil cooler housing
28 Ejector exhaust stubs
29 Cowling gills
30 Engine bearers

31 Oil tank (50 litre/11 Imp gal capacity)
32 Vent
33 Gun cooling muffle
34 Firewall/bulkhead
35 Ho-103 machine-gun (two) of 13mm calibre
36 Main fuel tank (217 litre/47.7 Imp gal capacity)
37 Port ammunition tank (350 rounds)
38 Fuel filler cap
39 Rudder pedals
40 Control column
41 Instrument panel
42 Fuselage flush-riveted stressed-skin panels
43 Reflector sight (offset to starboard)
44 Armour glass (65mm) windscreen
45 Aft-sliding cockpit canopy
46 Canopy lock/release
47 Pilot's headrest
48 Pilot's head armour/turnover support
49 Canopy fixed aft glazing
50 Canopy track
51 Entry handgrip
52 Pilot's 13mm back armour
53 Elevator trim handwheel
54 Pilot's seat (adjustable vertically)
55 Throttle quadrant
56 Flap setting lever
57 Undercarriage selector lever
58 Underfloor control runs
59 Flap-rod linkage
60 Water-methanol tank
61 Mid-fuselage construction break

62 Radio equipment tray
63 Type 4 Hi no.3 radio communications pack
64 Aerial lead-in
65 Aerial mast
66 Aerials
67 Light alloy semi-monocoque fuselage structure
68 Fuselage upper longeron
69 Oval section fuselage aft frames
70 Aft fuselage construction break
71 Starboard tailplane
72 Elevator balance
73 Starboard elevator (fabric covered)
74 Elevator trim tab
75 Tailfin leading edge
76 Tailfin structure
77 Rear navigation/ formation light
78 Aerial stub attachment
79 Rudder upper hinge
80 Rudder frame (fabric covered)
81 Rudder trim tab
82 Rudder centre hinge
83 Rudder lower section
84 Elevator trim tab
85 Elevator frame (fabric covered)
86 Tailplane structure
87 Tailwheel doors
88 Solid rubber tyre
89 Aft-retracting tailwheel
90 Fuselage lower longeron
91 Tail surface control cables
92 Oxygen cylinders
93 Radio access

94 Retractable entry step
95 Wing root fairing
96 Fairing former
97 Port main wing tank (173 litre/40 Imp gal capacity)
98 Fuel filler cap
99 Wing spar
100 Undercarriage leg cut-outs
101 Mainwheel wells
102 Mainwheel doors
103 Port 20mm Ho-5 cannon muzzle
104 Wheel brake hydraulic lines
105 Shock-absorber links
106 Port mainwheel
107 Axle
108 Mainwheel leg fairing
109 Underwing auxiliary fuel tank (200 litres/44 Imp gal capacity)
110 Landing light
111 Cannon blast tube
113 Flap tracks
114 Flap track extension fairings
115 Fowler-type flap structure
116 Rear auxiliary spar
117 Cannon ammunition tank (150 rounds)
118 Spar join
119 Port auxiliary leading-edge tank (67 litre/14.7 Imp gal capacity)
120 Fuel filler cap
121 Pitot tube
123 Main spar outer section
124 Wing ribs
125 Aileron control rod link fairing
126 Aileron trim tab

127 Aileron frame (fabric covered)
128 Wing skinning
129 Port wingtip
130 Port navigation light

SPECIFICATION Ki-84-Ia

Type

Single-seat interceptor fighter/fighter-bomber

Powerplant

One 1416kW (1900hp) Nakajima Ha-45 radial piston engine

Performance

Maximum speed: 631km/h (392mph) at 6120m (20,080ft); service ceiling: 10,500m (34,350ft); maximum range: 2168km (1347 miles)

Weights

Empty: 5864lb (2660kg); maximum take-off: 8576lb (3890kg)

Dimensions

Wingspan: 11.24m (36ft 10.5in); length: 9.92m (32ft 6.5in); height: 3.39m (11ft 1.5in); wing area: 21.00m² (226sqft)

Armament

Two 12.7mm (0.5in) machine-guns and two 20mm cannon, plus underwing racks for two 250kg (551lb) bombs

This Ki-106 prototype was built very late in the war. Although it looked like the Ki-84, it was made entirely of wood – in an attempt to save strategic materials.

This cutaway shows the Nakajima Ki-84-Ia Ko, the most widely produced version of the 'Dinah'. It was armed with two 12.7mm Ho-103 machine guns and two 20mm Ho-5 cannons in the wings.

Bibliography

Dyer, Edwin M. *Japanese Secret Projects 2 X-Planes and Experimental Aircraft of the IJA and IJN 1922–1945*, Crecy, 2014

Edwards, Peter J. *The Rise and Fall of the Japanese Imperial Naval Air Service*, Pen & Sword, 2010

Holmes, Tony (Editor). *Dogfight – The Greatest Air Duels of World War II*, Osprey, 2011

Ichimura, Hiroshi. *Ki-43 Oscar Aces of World War 2*, Osprey, 2009

Ishiguro, Ryusuke and Tadeusz Januszewski. *Kugisho E14Y Glen – The Aircraft That Bombed America*, Mushroom Model Publications, 2012

Marsh, Don and Peter Starkings. *Imperial Japanese Army Flying Schools 1912–1945*, Schiffer, 2011

Millman, Nicholas. *Ki-44 Tojo Aces of World War 2*, Osprey, 2011

Molesworth, Carl. *P-40 Warhawk vs Ki-43 Oscar: China 1944–45*, Osprey, 2008

Nedialkov, Dimitar. *In The Skies Of Nomonhan – Japan versus Russia May–September 1939*, Crecy Publishing, 2005

Nijboer, Donald. *P-38 Lightning vs Ki-61 Tony: New Guinea 1943–44*, Osprey, 2010

Nijboer, Donald. *Seafire vs A6M Zero: Pacific Theatre*, Osprey, 2009

Sakaida, Henry, Gary Nila and Koji Takaki. *I-400 – Japan's Secret Aircraft-Carrying Strike Submarine*, Flight Recorder Publications, 2006

Smith, Peter C. *Kamikaze – To Die for the Emperor*, Pen & Sword, 2014

Stewart, Adrian. *Carriers at War 1939–1945*, Pen & Sword, 2013

Toland, John. *The Rising Sun – The Decline and Fall of the Japanese Empire, 1936–1945*, Pen & Sword, 1971 (2011)

Treadwell, Terry C. *The Setting Of The Rising Sun – Japanese Military Aviation, 1877–1945*, Amberley Publishing, 2010

Werneth, Ron. *Beyond Pearl Harbor – The Untold Stories of Japan's Naval Airmen*, Schiffer, 2008

Wieliczko, Leszeck. *Japanese Fighters In Defense of the Homeland, 1941–1944* (Volume I), Kagero, 2014

Wieliczko, Leszeck. *Kawasaki Ki-61 Hien & Ki-100*, Kagero, 2015

Wieliczko, Leszeck. *Nakajima Ki-84 Hayate*, Kagero, 2013

Young, Edward M. *B-24 Liberator vs Ki-43 Oscar: China and Burma 1943*, Osprey, 2012

Zaloga, Steven J. *Kamikaze – Japanese Special Attack Weapons 1944–45*, Osprey, 2011

In addition to the above, which were all still available at the time of writing, the author made use of the extensive work of René J. Francillon, most of which is now out of print, including: *Japanese Aircraft of the Pacific War* (Putnam, 1987), *Japanese Navy Bombers of World War Two* (Doubleday, 1971), *Japanese Carrier Air Groups, 1941–45* (with Terry Hadler, Osprey, 1979) and his contributions to the *Aircraft Profile* (Profile Publications) series.

Index